DOMINATE LIFE

How to Get Clarity, Find Your Passion, and Live a Life You Love

KEARA PALMAY

ISBN: 978-1-5369-2003-1

This book is dedicated to my father,
Richard Leo Palmay.

You are the driving force
behind everything I do.

Knowing that you are smiling
down at me from Heaven inspires me
to become a better woman.

You brought me life,
From a seed.
Since I am you,
You live through me.

I couldn't have done this without you.
Thank you.

I love you.

*This book is also dedicated to you,
the reader.*

*All of the profits from Dominate Life are donated to
the Make-A-Wish Foundation.*

*The Make-A-Wish Foundation grants wishes to
children with cancer; they transform dreams into a
reality.*

*This is exactly what Dominate Life will do for you—
transform your dreams into a reality.*

*Thank you for your generous donation to the Make-
A-Wish Foundation and for your ambition to dream.*

You make a difference.

TABLE OF CONTENTS

FOREWORD	*V*
INTRODUCTION	*VII*
1. YOUR NEGATIVE BRAIN, DEMYSTIFIED	5
2. THE GIFT IS IN THE SHIT	12
3. NOW IS IT.	25
4. DON'T HATE: APPRECIATE	32
5. THE SUBCONSCIOUS MIND	42
6. THE LANGUAGE OF LASTING CHANGE	54
7. CHANGE YOUR IDENTITY	66
8. RITUALS TO RUN THE GAME	73
9. TO SEE IS TO BELIEVE.	79
10. DECIDE TO DOMINATE.	86
11. DO YOU.	87
12. YOUR PURPOSE DEBUNKED	93
13. YOUR MISSION DEFINED	97
14. ELIMINATE EXCUSES	114
15. GET A COACH	120

16. PEER GROUP   **125**

17. IT'S PARTY TIME   **129**

18. OFF INTO THE WILD   **132**

19. MY GIFT TO YOU   **137**

ABOUT KEARA   **141**

FOREWORD

THANK YOU for making an investment in this book and supporting the Make-A-Wish Foundation. It is a cause that is very close to my heart. *Dominate Life: How to Get Clarity, Find Your Passion, and Live a Life You Love* contains a wealth of powerful resources that will rock your world; I am so excited to share this journey with you.

When I hear the name Keara Palmay, so many wonderful things come to mind. I have an immense level of love for this woman and everything she represents. She is not only one of my closest friends, but an extremely ambitious business partner and a co-creator towards living an incredible life.

Ever since I met Keara, she's had an intense fire in her eyes and a burning passion to impact the world. I knew that she was onto something big, yet I don't think she knew exactly what that was. Despite her lack of clarity, I knew she was going to leave a massive imprint on the world no matter what. That's exactly what she's doing now.

Over the years, I've watched Keara evolve in a powerful way. It brings me such joy to witness her blossoming. I know for a fact that anything she does is of the utmost value—that's why I'm extremely honored to write the foreword for her first book. This is the beginning of an incredible journey.

For quite some time, Keara has shared her writing with me and it's moved me in a way that no other author has. What you will experience in *Dominate Life* is art in its purest form; it's a masterpiece that will change your life in an ardent way. I've read this book numerous times and each time it gave me a new breakthrough. It gives me the ability to look at life in a way that I've never envisioned before.

The great Marcel Proust, once said

"The real voyage of discovery consists not in seeking new landscapes, but in having new eyes."

After reading this book, you will have a new set of eyes along with a new action plan to live your absolute best life! Be prepared for a paradigm shift that will rock your world...

AJ Mihrzad,
Best Selling Author, *The Mind Body Solution*
Founder of OnlineSuperCoach.com
Attract, Sell and Serve Like a Million Dollar Online Coach

Introduction

Disclaimer: This book is the unfiltered, uncut Keara Palmay. What this means is that I'm blunt, I swear, and I share wildly stupid things that I've done in the past with the intention of empowering you to become the best version of yourself (regardless of who you used to be). **Now is all that matters.**

I WAS ONLY sixteen when I was diagnosed with cancer. I didn't know what to think of it. Naturally, I was curious, *why me?* I didn't believe in God, but I started to assume He was punishing me for one of two reasons.

The first reason God might have punished me was because I wasn't a Believer. I never saw the point in going to church every Sunday morning or saying my Hail Marys each night. My mom forced me to attend youth group meetings at our local Catholic Church, but I hid in the bathroom during each meeting. If anyone asked, I said I had diarrhea. I did this so frequently that I developed a reputation as "the girl with the runs." Everyone in the youth group stopped talking to me because they were concerned I might soil my pants mid-conversation. Mission accomplished.

The second reason God might have punished me was because the day prior to my cancer diagnosis, I smoked copious amounts of marijuana and accidentally ran over my neighbor's mailbox. I didn't tell anyone about this until now. Sorry, if you're reading this, Kathy. Your replacement mailbox looks stunning.

Whether or not there was any reason behind my cancer diagnosis, something profound shifted within me that day. It felt as though my mind, body, and spirit were illuminated with infinite light. It might sound "woo-woo," but I experienced an inexplicable sense of awakening that day.

I can't tell you what it was that "woke me up." It wasn't the annoying beeping machines. It wasn't the visitors who nervously looked at me like I was a living corpse. It wasn't the priest who administered Anointing of the Sick as if God were about to steal me from my hospital bed and never bring me back. It certainly wasn't the IV team who repetitively blew my veins and made me look like a complete junkie. No. It was something much greater than all of that; it was something much greater than myself. Amidst all of the chaos, something inside of me shifted in an ethereal way that words cannot express. I knew my life would never be the same again.

From that point forward, I knew I needed to make a difference in the world while I had the privilege of being alive. I realized that in order to change the world, I needed to change myself first. I worked around the clock to restore my health until I was stronger and more vibrant than some of the healthiest people I've ever met. It wasn't easy, but I'm proud to say I kicked cancer's ass (and then some).

After I restored my health, I felt vibrant yet emotionally overwhelmed; I couldn't help but question the meaning of my life. I was determined to discover my purpose and to empower others to do the same. I was a woman on a mission to change the world!

Doors began opening for me once I took massive action towards my mission. People noticed that I had insane amounts of energy along with an undeniable eagerness to serve. Today, I am very blessed to be an entrepreneur and a professional Results Coach for a major organization. I've learned from some of the most influential leaders in the world. Simply put, I maximize people's greatness and inspire them into action. I am so passionate about the work I do; it's the reason why I exist!

I wrote this book to share the fundamental principles that will help you live life on your terms. "Dominating life" simply means that *you* call the shots by creating your life's blueprint and actively building it into existence.

If you've ever said to yourself, *"There's got to be more to life than this..."* then *Dominate Life* is the book for you. The truth is, no one will wave a magic wand over your head and make your dreams come true; it's 100% your responsibility. *You* are the only one in the driver's seat of your life, so you need a clear understanding of where you're going before you can show up. If you don't know where you're going or you keep changing your destination, you will always be lost.

Dominate Life will help you find your way. In fact, as you read this book and participate in the activities, your standards will raise so high that you will never look back again!

Imagine how liberating it will feel when you completely break through the limits that have held you back in the past. What will be possible when you truly live up to your full potential? What will it mean to you to finally start creating the passionate and purpose-driven life you deserve? How will this change your life and the lives of the people you love? What doors will open for you? Fortunately, the key to those doors is in your hands right now!

Dominate Life is an interactive workbook, meaning your participation is required. It's time to break the cycle of passivity and take a stand for the incredible life you deserve. The results you produce from this book will be a direct reflection of the effort you put into the activities, so it's imperative that you take action!

If you own the electronic version of this book, please download the workbook and print it out.

You can download your workbook here: www.kearapalmay.com/workbook.

Put your thinking cap on, grab a pen, and gear up for one of the most transformative journeys of your life—*Dominate Life*!

1

YOUR NEGATIVE BRAIN, DEMYSTIFIED

"We can complain because rose bushes have thorns, or rejoice because thorn bushes have roses."
—Abraham Lincoln

EVER CATCH YOURSELF complaining for no apparent reason at all? Perhaps it's too cold outside, or maybe the sun isn't shining bright enough. Perhaps you're too hungry to chitchat with your waiter; you want your damn waffles right now. Maybe your dad showed up to breakfast wearing that douchey turtleneck that's haunted you since 1996. Ugh, when is he going to get rid of that thing?!

If this sounds like you at times, you're actually normal. In fact, so many of us complain without even realizing we're doing it. I used to complain for the vast majority of my life until I realized that I was contributing to my own misery.

Despite this realization, however, I still caught myself complaining. I tried my best to suppress my complaints, yet they seemed to burst out of me like pent-up sneezes. They were the kind of sneezes that felt really good, too. I began to wonder why I got such a sick thrill out of complaining. I heard the phrase, "misery loves company," so I found comfort in the fact that I wasn't the only one behaving like a whiny little baby. I still wondered, though, *why is it that society as a whole tends to dwell upon negativity?* I decided to do some research.

I learned that **our brain is two million years old. It isn't designed to help us feel good—it's designed to help us survive**.

To apply this concept to the real world, let's travel back in time to the Paleolithic era. Think about it, if our ancestors were walking through the woods and an object swiftly moved beneath their feet, they had to quickly determine whether that object was a snake or a stick. If they assumed it was a stick, they *might* flee and *might* survive. However, if the object *were* a snake, they *might* die. Thus, in order to survive, our ancestors had to assume the worst and flee—even if they were running from a measly stick. This explains why humans are literally programmed to experience more negative emotions than positive; it's helped us survive as a species.

Similarly, if our ancestors ate berries that made them sick, their mind would associate berries with illness. Because of that one bad experience, they would never eat those berries again; it meant life or death to them. This is how negative thinking has helped us survive. This explains why you're not a jerk if you're a whiny complainer like I was.

Although our world is profoundly less dangerous today than it was for our ancestors, our minds still respond to stressors the same way they did in the past. The major difference now is that we aren't running from life or death situations—we are running from our emotions.

For example, many people whom have gone through divorces associate love with pain. Therefore, many of them avoid falling in love again because they don't want to get hurt. This is similar to the example of the berries; when our ancestors ate berries that made them sick, they would avoid them at all costs. Nowadays, if a woman associates love with pain, for example, she avoids love at all costs. Her fears will influence her behavior and cause her to experience difficulty falling in love—whether she's consciously aware of it or not.

Research supports that a negativity bias is a real thing. In the Ohio State University study *Negative Information Weighs More Heavily on the Brain: The Negative Bias in Evaluative Categorizations,* study participants were shown pictures known to elicit positive feelings (like a Lamborghini or ice cream), negative feelings (like a car crash or a bloody face), and neutral feelings (like a toothpick or a blank sheet of paper). The researchers studied the participants' neurological responses to the stimuli and concluded that the brain responds to negative stimuli with far greater intensity than positive. Additionally, they found that negative stimuli are more likely to elicit sympathetic activation as part of an adaptive fight-or-flight response.[1]

This goes to show that even when you experience stress from something as trivial as a traffic jam, you experience the same biochemical response that your ancestors did as they ran from predators. This happens because your mind and body perceive stressful situations as life or death situations. When this happens, you go into fight or flight mode and secrete a cocktail of taxing stress hormones like cortisol, norepinephrine, and adrenaline. Sounds pretty unnecessary for all of that to happen over a meager traffic jam, right?

To dominate life, you need to get rid of old programming that doesn't serve you. If you want to feel more fulfilled, the easiest thing to do is quit bitching! Whenever you catch yourself complaining from here on out, pause, take a deep breath, and start over. Say whatever you want to say without complaining.

To take it to the next level, it's advantageous to reframe your complaints. The activity below will give you the opportunity to make light of the things you regularly complain about. You might even start

---

[1]Ito, Tiffany A., et al. "Negative Information Weighs More Heavily on the Brain: The Negativity Bias in Evaluative Categorizations." *Journal of Personality and Social Psychology* 75.4 (1998): 887-900. Print.

to laugh at how ridiculous your complaints have been.

If you do not have the paperback version of this book, please download the *Dominate Life* workbook and print it out now. You will only reap the maximum benefits of this book when you participate in the activities.

You can download your workbook here: www.kearapalmay.com/workbook

Activity:

List 3 things you complain about regularly.
For example, you might say, "I hate my job."

1.
My Car sucks.

2.
I hate traffic.

3.
My job is a waste of my time.

What could you appreciate about each complaint that could benefit you moving forward?

Example: If your complaint is that you hate your job, you could appreciate that your job gave you the experience you needed to move on to the next step in your life. You could appreciate the fact that you wouldn't be in a position to take the next step if you didn't master the skillsets at your current position. You could appreciate fact that your job helped you develop a sense of confidence in your area of expertise.

1.

My car was inexpensive and has never truly broken down. She's sizable and has cushy leather seats. I own her outright.

2.

Traffic gives me time alone in my day. I think and listen to music and audio books

3.

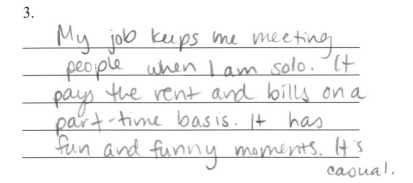

My job keeps me meeting
people when I am solo. It
pays the rent and bills on a
part-time basis. It has
fun and funny moments. It's
casual.

Now that you've learned that your mind can be a cynical little bastard, the next step is learning how to use it to elicit states of fulfillment, pleasure, and joy rather than misery. You'll have the opportunity to do this in the next chapter.

The bottom line is, your brain is plastic, meaning it has the capacity to change the way it's programmed. You are therefore in complete control of the way that your mind operates.

You might be thinking that after all of these years of developing your mind it's impossible to start thinking differently now. Fortunately, I'm not here to "reprogram" you; I'm here to help you maximize your potential by bringing out the best of what already exists within you. This process can begin whenever you choose—no matter how young or old you are.

Once you take control of your mind, you take control of your life. **Your life is merely a representation of whatever you *think* it is**—this can be your heaven, or this can be your Hell.

2.

THE GIFT IS IN THE SHIT

"You don't overcome challenges by making them smaller but by making yourself bigger."
—John C. Maxwell

IF YOU FEEL like your past is weighing you down, you're not alone. Everyone has experienced pain in the past, but pain is relative depending upon how you perceive it. This popular personal development story puts it into perspective very well:

A young southern man shot a convenience store clerk and went to prison. His wife was pregnant with twins. About thirty years later, a journalist tracked down the twins to see what they were doing with their lives. One of the twins grew up to become a successful attorney while the other twin was in prison for armed robbery—similar to his father. The journalist asked both of the twins the same question,

"How did you end up this way?" Both twins answered the same way, "With a father like that, how could I turn out any differently?"

You see, one of the twins created a belief system that, "because of my dad I *can't* succeed," while the other twin believed, "because of my dad, I *must* succeed."

This goes to show that you can't control the challenges in your life, but you *can* control what they mean to you. The most profound way to reframe past challenges is to remember that life happens *for* you, not *to* you. With that being said, **there are no victims in life.**

Victims are people who don't take responsibility for their actions; they believe that something outside of themselves determine their life conditions. They often blame someone or something else for their circumstances. Victims always have a victim story.

If you're a fan of sitting around the bonfire sharing sob stories about your life, then you're a victim. In order to break this pattern, you'll need to change your story. The major challenge with victims, however, is that they tend to defend their story like it's their first-born child. The reason they hang on to their story is because it helps them avoid taking responsibility for their circumstances. For example, as long as they blame the government for the fact that they don't make money, then they don't have to take responsibility to make money themselves.

If you have a victim story of your own, you must understand that you're the one holding onto it; no one can make you let it go. You must realize, however, that there are consequences to holding on to your story. The bottom line is, **you can't start a new story if you keep re-reading the last one.**

No matter how bad you think you have it, there is always someone who has it worse. You are not a victim unless you decide to be one. You can have whatever seemingly "tragic" personal history, but **your life circumstances boil down to the decisions you make.**

Everything in life has happened for a reason. It has led you to where you are right here, right now. **The biggest mistake we make in life is believing that there are mistakes.** There are no mistakes. Whatever has happened to you in life has led you to this pivotal moment right here, right now. Any other step could have taken you in a radically different direction. **Breathe. You are in the exact right place at the exact right time.**

Activity:

Rewrite this phrase 5 times on the lines below:
"I am in the exact right place at the exact right time."

I am in the exact right place at the exact right time.

I am in the exact right place at the exact right time

I am in the exact right place at the exact right time.

14

I am in the exact right place at the exact right time.
I am in the exact right place at the exact right time.

Yes, you are.

With that being said, however, if you're in pain, don't mitigate it. I don't say this to torture you; I say this because there's actually a lot of power to being in pain. **Pain is energy.** Think about it, people don't transform their lives when they're comfortable; when they're comfortable, they simply coast along. Most of the greatest transformations take place when people hit rock bottom. Once they hit rock bottom, they reach a threshold where they absolutely *cannot* tolerate the pain any longer. Pain is a great gift because it creates momentum; it lights a fire under your ass to raise your standards and to raise them immediately!

...So if you have a sob story, you can transform your character from a *victim* to a *victor* by channeling your pain into energy and using that energy to make a difference. You can do this by answering a few simple questions.

Activity:

1. What is something important that you've avoided taking responsibility for *(i.e., something that has been weighing on your consciousness)*?

_____

_____

_____

_____

_____

_____

2. Why haven't you taken responsibility yet?

_____

_____

_____

_____

_____

_____

_____

Realize that the reason "why" you've avoided taking responsibility is a complete story that you've made up. What I mean by this is, anytime you justify what you want by making excuses about why you don't have it (for example, anytime you say "I want X but Y..."), you're creating a bullshit story that keeps you small.

For example, one of my clients had a dream to become a veterinarian but he allowed his bullshit story of "not having enough money to go to school" prevent him from pursuing it. He was in massive pain when he enrolled in coaching because he felt like he gave up on his dream.

First off, let's be clear: I'm not saying he didn't have money. He could have been dead broke for all I knew. But the bottom line is, **when you want something bad enough, you'll find a way to make it happen.** Once he realized his story was limiting his growth, he let it go. He entered our second call with a list of ways he could earn money to go to school. He is now in the second year of a prestigious veterinarian program and is feeling more fulfilled than ever. This goes to show that you can change your story in an instant. When you change your story, your whole life changes. We'll get into rewriting your story later, but for now, let's focus on the power of pain again.

Pain is an incredible tool to help you discover your passion because pain yields empathy. Empathy is the ability to understand and share someone else's emotions. Here's a great metaphor to put it into perspective.

When you've been in pain, it's almost as if you've been in a dark hole. You might struggle to find your way out of that hole for days, weeks, months, or years, but you can eventually find your way out if you choose. Once you find your way out of the hole, you can help other people find their way out, too. You simply jump down to the bottom of the hole, take the person's hand, and guide them out because you already know the way.

Empathy is your greatest gift when it comes to discovering your purpose—when you understand someone's struggle, you tend to have a genuine desire to help. This wouldn't take place if you coasted through life with ease. That's why it's often the most challenging circumstances in your life that will help you discover your deepest-rooted passion.

Think about it, how have the challenges you've overcome helped you evolve as a person? How can you empower other people because of that experience?

Activity:

Write down the 3 biggest challenges you've been through in life along with what you've learned from them, how they've made you a better person, and how you can use your wisdom from these experiences to make a difference.

First challenge:

_____

_____

_____

_____

_____

_____

_____

What I learned from it:

_____

_____

_____

_____

_____

_____

_____

How it made me a better person:

_____

_____

_____

_____

_____

_____

_____

How I can make a difference because of this experience:

_____

_____

_____

_____

_____

_____

_____

Second challenge:

_____

_____

_____

_____

_____

_____

_____

What I learned from it:

_____

_____

_____

_____

_____

_____

_____

How it made me a better person:

_____

_____

_____

_____

_____

_____

_____

How I can make a difference because of this experience:

_____

_____

_____

_____

_____

_____

_____

Third challenge:

_____

_____

_____

_____

_____

_____

_____

What I learned from it:

_____

_____

_____

_____

_____

_____

_____

_____

How it made me a better person:

_____

_____

_____

_____

_____

_____

_____

_____

How I can make a difference because of this experience:

_____

_____

_____

_____

_____

_____

_____

_____

3.

NOW IS IT.

"The only true thing is what's in front of you right now."
—Ramona Ausubel

TO DOMINATE life, the first place to begin is the present moment. The power of living in the present moment seems so elementary, yet **most people suffer because they chase the bright, shiny objects rather than mastering the fundamentals.** What's even more powerful than living in the present moment is actually *enjoying* the present moment. We'll discuss how to do that in this chapter.

Like we've discussed, most people are unfulfilled because they feel weighed down by the past. They allow past experiences to shape their lives as if those experiences will continue to happen in the future. They might say things like "I can never love again because my ex-husband abused me," or

"I will never succeed because I never got accepted to college," or "I will never be healthy because I've been having a love affair with pizza." People repeat stories from the past so frequently that they believe they're still true now and will continue to be true in the future. Like driving a car, **you can't move forward if you're looking in the rearview mirror.** You will crash!

Another reason why most people feel unfulfilled is because their future ideals dictate their feelings in the present moment. They say things like, "Once I get promoted, I will be happy," or "My life will be complete once I find a husband," or "I'll feel sexy once I lose 10 pounds," or "When I make a million dollars, I will live life to the fullest!" These are bullshit rules that create suffering because they are unattainable in the present moment. You came here to dominate life, so here's the real truth: **if you can't find something to appreciate now, you won't find something to appreciate later.**

Since you can't possibly live in the past or future, you can't possibly feel happiness if you believe it exists in a different place and time. All you have is this moment—right here, right now. To maximize your personal fulfillment, you must be able to find something to appreciate at all times.

The goal of this chapter is to become a Master of Reality, or someone who has the ability to accept something exactly the way it is with nothing added and nothing left out. This doesn't mean you're going to turn into a Monk and sit on a rock for the rest of your life; you still have to take action to get what you want. The reason why it's critical to master your reality is because once you're able to get a grip on your thoughts and feelings in the present moment, you'll get a grip on how to create any reality you desire.

How to Master Your Reality:

Humans have about 60-70,000 thoughts per day. We aren't even consciously aware of most of our thoughts yet they unconsciously dictate the direction of our focus, behavior, and lives.

For example, if you think, "I suck at sales," it will influence your behavior around sales, which will influence the results you produce, (i.e., you will most-likely bomb your sales calls). The worst part is, you might not even *realize* that you think you suck at sales, yet this subconscious belief has enough power to completely influence the world around you (your life).

Our thoughts shape our entire life! The formula is simple:

Think empowering thoughts→Live an empowering life.

--or--

Think disempowering thoughts → Live a disempowering life.

In order to experience greater fulfillment in each and every moment, you must become aware of what you tend to think about. Listen to your thoughts and notice what comes up. Do you hear yourself complaining? Do you hear yourself judging others? Do you hear yourself stressing about things that you can't control in the present moment?

Simply tune in and notice what's going on. It is very important not to judge your thoughts. Nothing will change if you start beating yourself over the head every time you experience a "bad" thought. Pay close attention to how you think—do your thoughts support you or make you miserable? Of course you won't (and probably *can't*) listen to all 60-70,000 thoughts per day, but make it a daily practice to turn inward and observe the patterns that show up in your mind.

Once you become aware of your thought patterns, you can replace the ones that don't empower you with ones that do. It's simple: when a disempowering thought enters your mind, acknowledge it and gently push it away. Think of the negative thought as though it were a bubble. Gently pop the bubble with a feather so it's gone forever; replace it with an empowering alternative that supports you in the moment.

All transformation begins with awareness. Before you can transform your mind, you must become aware that all of that noise in your head is *not* you. **Until you can distinguish yourself from the voice in your head, you cannot be present.**

Take charge of your mind by making it a daily commitment to turn inward and reframe your inner monologue.

For example, if you're thinking something like,

Why is Susan ignoring my calls? Is she upset with me? It's been five hours!

Replace the thought with one that surrenders control and accepts reality; you could think something like,

Susan is my best friend. I understand that she is a very busy woman and I respect her space. This conversation isn't urgent. She will get back to me at the perfect moment in time.

Do you notice how the first thought created suffering while the second completely accepted what "is?"

At first, it takes a great deal of focus to reframe your thoughts. It's similar to exercising at the gym; when you're new to the gym, your form seems awkward. After you go for a while, however, you become unconsciously competent (meaning you automatically know what you're doing without thinking about it). Similarly, reframing your thoughts seems awkward at first, but the more you do it, the more you eliminate suffering at the source.

The bottom line is, **if you can't solve a challenge in this moment, then no amount of worrying will solve it for you.** When you're present, you have one of two options: either take responsibility to solve a challenge in the moment or, when nothing can be done, peacefully release control and make better use of your time.

The truth is, our thoughts and feelings are much like the clouds in the sky; they constantly come and go. They are completely transient in nature and are therefore not to be taken so seriously. When you put it into that perspective, you will realize that disempowering thoughts don't simply go away. Since they don't go away, there is no point in expending your precious energy fighting them. Rather than fighting them, ask yourself, "who am I going to be in the face of my disempowering thoughts?" For example, if you are fearful to quit your job because you're afraid to fail, acknowledge your fear and ask, "Who am I going to be in the face of fear?" **Once you get a handle on your thoughts and emotions, they have no control over you anymore.**

A man is the sum of all of his thoughts, so when you dominate your thoughts, you dominate your life.

Activity:

Rewrite this phrase 5 times on the lines below:
"My thoughts don't run my life anymore; I do."

_____

_____

_____

_____

_____

_____

_____

_____

_____

_____

_____

4.

Don't Hate: Appreciate

"Be thankful for what you have; you'll end up having more. If you concentrate on what you don't have, you will never, ever have enough."
—Oprah Winfrey

GRATITUDE is such a simple yet powerful tool that is at our disposal at all times. Like I said before, if you can't find something to appreciate now, you won't find something to appreciate later. When you feel grateful, you don't take anything or anyone for granted; you appreciate everything as it is. When you appreciate what you already have, you end up with even more.

Here are some cool scientific facts about gratitude from Forbes.com:[2]

Gratitude improves psychological health. Gratitude reduces a multitude of toxic emotions, ranging from envy and resentment to frustration and regret. Robert A. Emmons, Ph.D., a leading gratitude researcher, has conducted multiple studies on the link between gratitude and well-being. His research confirms that gratitude effectively increases happiness and reduces depression.

Gratitude enhances empathy and reduces aggression. Grateful people are more likely to behave in a prosocial manner, even when others behave less kindly, according to a 2012 study by the University of Kentucky. Study participants who ranked higher on gratitude scales were less likely to retaliate against others, even when given negative feedback. They experienced more sensitivity and empathy toward other people and a decreased desire to seek revenge.

Gratitude improves self-esteem. A 2014 study published in the *Journal of Applied Sport Psychology* found that gratitude increased athlete's self-esteem, which is an essential component to optimal performance. Other studies have shown that gratitude reduces social comparisons. Rather

---

[2]Morin, Amy. "7 Scientifically Proven Benefits Of Gratitude That Will Motivate You To Give Thanks Year-Round." *Forbes.* 23 Nov. 2014. Web. 19 Jul. 2016.

than becoming resentful toward people who have more money or better jobs—which is a major factor in reduced self-esteem—grateful people are able to appreciate other people's accomplishments.

Gratitude increases mental strength. For years, research has shown gratitude not only reduces stress, but it may also play a major role in overcoming trauma. A 2006 study published in *Behavior Research and Therapy* found that Vietnam War Veterans with higher levels of gratitude experienced lower rates of Post-Traumatic Stress Disorder. A 2003 study published in the *Journal of Personality and Social Psychology* found that gratitude was a major contributor to resilience following the terrorist attacks on September 11th.

In order to feel grateful, start appreciating the little and big things that shape your life. You can feel grateful for anything—the sunshine on your skin, your mother's love, your ability to dream, a stranger's smile, etc. Whatever you choose to focus on is entirely up to you—just focus on whatever makes you feel good and you'll begin to feel even better.

How to Maximize Your Feelings of Gratitude:

Create a daily gratitude list each morning. Your brain still produces Alpha waves immediately after you wake up. Alpha waves bridge your conscious and unconscious minds; they can also be observed during deep states of mediation. What's cool about this is it's a great opportunity to receive honest guidance from your unconscious, dream-like mind. Once you're fully awake, your brain produces mostly Beta waves. This is when your conscious ego mind has a greater opportunity to chime in and poop on your party. Take advantage of your Alpha waves to amplify your feelings of clarity, joy, and appreciation for what "is" and what's to come.

Be sure not to check your phone or do anything else prior to or during reflecting. Simply meditate on your daily gratitudes and write them down. Russel Simmons says, "When I start my day by reflecting on all the things I have to be grateful for, I'll have a much more rewarding day."

Feeling grateful for each moment is such a simple yet powerful way to condition happiness. When you think about what you're grateful for, you naturally feel good. As a result, you get to shine more of your bright light onto the world.

Last chapter, we discussed how to enjoy the present moment. The most powerful way to enjoy the present moment is to appreciate everything and everyone that is shaping it.

As challenges show up in your life, find something to appreciate about them. Instead of getting upset, **ask each challenge *what are you here to teach me?*** Since gratitude is the antidote to frustration, you'll feel your worries melt away as soon as you shift your focus from expectation to appreciation.

Activity:

List 10 things you're grateful for now (big or small).

1._____

_____

2._____

_____

3._____

_____

4._____

_____

5._____

_____

6._____

_____

7._____

_____

8._____

_____

9._____

_____

10._____

_____

Next, list 5 things that have been frustrating you followed by something you could appreciate about them now.

What was frustrating me:

_____

_____

_____

_____

_____

_____

_____

What I can appreciate about it now:

_____

_____

_____

_____

_____

_____

_____

What was frustrating me:

_____

_____

_____

_____

_____

_____

_____

What I can appreciate about it now:

_____

_____

_____

_____

_____

_____

_____

What was frustrating me:

_____

_____

_____

_____

_____

_____

_____

What I can appreciate about it now:

_____

_____

_____

_____

_____

_____

_____

What was frustrating me:

_____

_____

_____

_____

_____

_____

_____

What I can appreciate about it now:

_____

_____

_____

_____

_____

_____

_____

What was frustrating me:

_____

_____

_____

_____

_____

_____

_____

What I can appreciate about it now:

_____

_____

_____

_____

_____

_____

Don't you feel so much better now? Look at all of the things there are to appreciate in your life. Once you reframe your mind to notice what you can appreciate about each moment, your levels of fulfillment will go through the roof!

5.

THE SUBCONSCIOUS MIND

"Whatever we plant in our subconscious mind and nourish with repetition and emotion will one day become a reality."
—Earl Nightingale

HAVE YOU EVER had a completely random song stuck in your head and had no idea how it got there? The reason you don't know how the song got stuck in your head is because it happened unconsciously. Your subconscious mind is responsible for situations like this.

The subconscious mind is the part of the brain that is functioning at all times. It's causing your heart to beat as you read this. It's helping you breathe without thinking. It picks up the sensory information from everything taking place within and around you, like the scents, sights, sounds, sensations, feelings, and experiences that collectively create your life.

Thus, everything you experience enters your brain and leaves an impression on you whether you're consciously aware that it's happening or not. In fact, your subconscious mind is so powerful that researchers at the American Society of Anesthesiologists (ASA) found that rats' brains can learn and remember odors they were exposed to while under anesthesia.[3] Although the rats had no memory of being exposed to an odor, changes in brain tissue (particularly in the cerebellum, or "the smell brain") implied that the rats "remembered" the exposure to the unfamiliar odor. This suggests that our brain not only receives sensory information, but also registers information at an unconscious cellular level. The bottom line is, our subconscious mind never sleeps. This explains why we've all had songs stuck in our heads but had no idea where or when we even heard the song; we picked it up subconsciously.

Your brain is a complex machine. It has a lot to remember. Since your brain can't possibly remember everything, it filters most information (stimuli) out. You are therefore only consciously aware of a very small fraction of your experiences. The rest of the information gets stored in your subconscious mind.

---

[3]Sobell, Noam, et al. "Odorant-Induced and Sniff-Induced Activation in the Cerebellum of the Human." *The Journal of Neuroscience* 18.21 (1998): 8990-9001. Print.

Your subconscious mind contains infinite knowledge and it's just sitting there waiting for you to give it expression. It is very sensitive to the information it receives. It's like a bed of soil that accepts any information—good or bad. **Whatever types of thoughts you plant into your soil of consciousness emerge and take shape as an outer experience, which is your life.**

If you think good, good will follow; if you think bad, bad will follow. Your subconscious mind is like a three-year-old child. It does not judge the messages you send it. It simply accepts them as true and takes action to prove you right. To dominate life, you must program your mind to work in your favor.

People often limit themselves without realizing it. They create beliefs about what's possible based upon their past experiences. They store these beliefs inside a box, which represents their reality. Anything outside of their reality is unknown. Since it's unknown, they have no references to understand what life is like outside of the box; it's like uncharted territory that seems unsafe to enter. Although it seems unsafe outside of the box, some of life's most incredible rewards exist there, like abundance, freedom, passion, etc.

People want to step outside of the box yet most of them experience major conflicts once they do. Simply put, feeling joyful for endured periods of time can seem incongruent with who they are. This perceived incongruence can cause massive amounts of uncertainty. If the uncertainty becomes unbearable enough, they'll regress back to their comfort zones. **People will sacrifice their deepest desires simply to experience the illusion of safety.**

For example, have you ever been in a relationship that was going so well that you thought *this is too good to be true*? Well, when you say *this is too good to be true*, you actually mean *this is too good to be consistent with who I am.* When this happens, you'll find ways to sabotage your relationship because your subconscious mind listens to your thoughts and acts on them accordingly. Thus, **when you believe something is too good to be true, your brain will prove you right.** You'll create problems in your relationship, business, body, or whatever, to return to your comfort zone.

Hendricks Gay, writer of *The Big Leap* calls this type of problem an "Upper Limit Problem." Upper Limit Problems take place when you feel so fulfilled that it almost scares you, so you create problems to keep you safe and small.

People often go through life recreating different problems with different circumstances that snap them back to the same comfort zone. This happens because familiarity is comfortable while uncharted territory isn't. Simply put, it's more comfortable to experience the devil you know than the devil you don't know.

Due to the subconscious mind, **whatever you focus on internally shows up externally**. A man named Sam Londe found this out the hard way. In 1974, Sam was diagnosed with cancer of the esophagus. His doctors surgically removed all of the cancer in his esophagus, but a scan of Londe's liver revealed that he had cancer throughout the entire left lobe. His doctors told him that this specific type of liver cancer was 100% fatal and there was no chance he would survive. Two months later, Sam died.[4]

You would think Sam died of cancer, but his autopsy shockingly revealed that his liver actually *wasn't* filled with cancer. There was only a tiny nodule of cancer on his liver and one small spot on his lung, but nothing that had enough power to kill him. Sam died because he *believed* he was going to die. Thus, **whatever you focus on and believe with emotional conviction becomes your life.** This is your heaven, or this is your Hell.

Everything that you have in life is a reflection of your beliefs because your beliefs influence your behavior and your behavior produces your results.

The model looks like this:
Beliefs → Behavior → Results

---

[4]Dispenza, Dr. Joe. "Can Thoughts Along Cause an Early Death?" *Heal Your Life.* Hay House, Inc. 30 Apr. 2014. Web. 19 Jul. 2016.

This model represents that your beliefs influence your behavior, which influence your results, which reinforce your beliefs.

Example
Belief: "I am going to fail my exam."

Behavior: Anxiety; trying to study but can't concentrate due to stress; discouraged from studying; *why even bother when I will just fail anyway?*

Results: Failed exam.

The end result thus "proves" your belief to be true. This is when you start saying things like, "See? I told ya so!" You will run through this cycle until you interrupt your pattern and adopt new beliefs.

If you aren't sure how your beliefs are shaping your reality, simply look at your results. What I mean when I say "look at your results" is to take a look at what's going on in your life. Look at your body. What are the results telling you? Look at your finances. What are the numbers telling you? Look at your relationships and any other areas of your life that are important to you. Assess the feedback. What are your results telling you? There's no such thing as good or bad results—results are just feedback. The truth is, **results don't lie.** Thankfully, if you don't like your results, you can change them.

...But before you can change your results, you must change your beliefs. If you think your results suck, it's because you have belief systems that don't support you. Conversely, if you think your results are great, it's because you have belief systems that do support you. Tony Robbins says, **"What's bad is always present and so is what's good. It's what you choose to focus on that you'll feel."**

The truth is, you're worthy of having it all. **Once you let go of the limited, the unlimited finally has room to exist.** It all begins by creating belief systems that empower you to step into your greatness. The best way to dominate life is to condition your subconscious mind to achieve what you believe—but you must first believe in empowering possibilities rather than disempowering limits.

Activity:

On a scale of 1-10, rate your level of fulfillment in each of the following areas of life (1 being completely unfulfilled, and 10 being completely fulfilled).

Health/Physical Body: _____
Relationships: _____
Finances: _____
Spirituality: _____

1. Which area of your life ranked the lowest on the fulfillment scale?

_____

What would you have to believe about yourself to raise that number to a 10?

_____

_____

_____

_____

_____

_____

_____

_____

Write the words, "I choose to believe this is true NOW."

_____

_____

In order to raise that number to a 10, what would you do differently? Meaning, what would you do that you're not doing now?

_____

_____

_____

_____

_____

Now write the words, "I am committed to doing this NOW."

_____

_____

Condition these beliefs and actions until they become part of your identity.

2. Which area of your life ranked the lowest on the fulfillment scale?

_____

What would you have to believe about yourself to raise that number to a 10?

_____

_____

_____

_____

_____

_____

_____

Write the words, "I choose to believe this is true NOW."

_____

_____

In order to raise that number to a 10, what would you do differently? Meaning, what would you do that you're not doing now?

_____

_____

_____

_____

_____

_____

_____

Now write the words, "I am committed to doing this NOW."

_____

_____

Condition these beliefs and actions until they become part of your identity.

3. Which area of your life ranked the lowest on the fulfillment scale?

_____

What would you have to believe about yourself to raise that number to a 10?

_____

_____

_____

_____

_____

_____

_____

Write the words, "I choose to believe this is true NOW."

_____

_____

In order to raise that number to a 10, what would you do differently? Meaning, what would you do that you're not doing now?

_____

_____

_____

_____

_____

_____

_____

Now write the words, "I am committed to doing this NOW."

_____

_____

Condition these beliefs and actions until they become part of your identity.

6.

THE LANGUAGE OF LASTING CHANGE

"Eliminate the word 'try' and see how much more you DO."
—*Keara Palmay*

SINCE YOUR SUBCONSCIOUS mind listens to your thoughts and environment at all times, it's important to be mindful of the language you use.

Language creates your world, so **when you say something like it's real, it becomes real**. For example, if you label yourself as an introvert, you will behave like one and consequently experience difficulty creating new and lasting relationships. If you label yourself as an addict, you'll behave like an addict. I'm not saying addiction isn't real, but I am saying that you must consider how the labels you use influence your reality. If the labels you empower you, that's fantastic. If not, why are you using them? Be mindful with your speaking. **Your language creates your reality.**

It's important to **speak into existence that which you choose to become.** This principle seems obvious, yet most people are programmed to talk about what they don't want. As a result, they keep creating more of what they don't want. This happens because **where focus goes, energy flows**. To dominate life, you must use language that tells your subconscious mind exactly what you *do* want rather than what you *don't*.

When I start working with new clients, for example, the first question I ask is *what do you want?* This totally throws them off. Most people can't answer. Instead, they ask questions like, "Well, what do you mean what do I want? You mean as a job? Do you mean in life? What do you mean what do I want?"

Unfortunately, most people seldom get what they want because they genuinely don't know. They're so focused on what they *don't* want, which explains why the same problems keep showing with different faces.

Let's run through a brief activity. The directions are simple: all you have to do is *not* think about a pink elephant. Pause for a brief moment and do everything in your power to avoid thinking about a pink elephant. Make sure that as you pause, you do not think about a pink elephant. After you pause, continue reading—without thinking about a pink elephant.

What happened when I told you not to think about a pink elephant? You probably saw the image of a pink elephant flash into your head, didn't you? And I told you *not* to think about a pink elephant!

This happens because our brain thinks in terms of shapes and symbols. The reticular activating system (RAS) is responsible for this. The RAS is the part of your brain that filters information into visual formations. Simply put, your RAS creates pictures for the language you use. The images that your RAS create give direction to your subconscious mind.

For example, imagine you want to buy a new car; we'll say it's a black 2016 Honda Civic. Part of the reason you enjoy the car so much is because you haven't seen many on the road yet; the car seems unique to you. Once you purchase the car, however, all of that changes. You begin to notice more and more black 2016 Honda Civics on the road. This doesn't happen because Honda mass-produced millions of the same car overnight; this happens because your RAS identifies with being the owner of a black 2016 Honda Civic and preferentially focuses on them. The bottom line is, **your mind is attracted to whatever you focus on.**

Thus, if you only focus on and identify with all of the things that you *don't* want in life, you'll end up getting more of what you don't want—because your brain is attracted to whatever you focus on.

To dominate life, you must use language that attracts what you want *specifically*. You can't hit a target you can't see. The more specific you are about your goals, the greater chance you have of hitting them.

When you say things like...
- "I don't want to be fat!"
- "I'm too broke to buy those shoes."

Your RAS sees mental images of *fat* and *broke,* and will therefore attract more fatness and brokeness. If you do succeed to lose weight or earn money, it's only a matter of time before you experience an Upper Limit Problem and self-sabotage your way back to your comfort zone.

On the contrast, when you say things like...
- "I get healthier each day."
- "I love money because it represents the value I share with the world."

Your RAS creates mental images of health and abundance and therefore attract more of it. Using this type of language gives you the opportunity to transform your identity to become someone who produces health and wealth.

Another important note is to speak in terms of positives, not negatives. Again, say what you want; not what you don't want. For example, if your kids are jumping on the couch like rabid animals, *don't* yell, "Stop jumping on the couch!" If you yell at them to stop jumping on the couch, their RAS will see the visual "jumping on the couch," which will subconsciously influence them to continue jumping on the couch. Remember when I told you *not* to think about a pink elephant but you did it anyway? The same principle applies here.

To communicate effectively, flip your negative commands to positive commands. In this situation, you could say something like, "I *want* you to sit down and color in your new coloring books." This gives the children a crystal clear direction of where to go and what to do because their subconscious mind will hear and see the visual of "sitting down and coloring in their new coloring books."

Also, there's a few words or phrases you should totally eliminate from your vocabulary...

— **Replace the words "have to" with "get to."**

o   For example, instead of saying, "I *have to* exercise today," replace it with, "I *get to* exercise today."

o   This makes the action sound like a privilege rather than a chore.

— **Replace the words "I can't" with either "I won't" or "I choose to...instead."**

o   For example, instead of saying "I *can't* afford to buy that shirt," you could say, "I *won't* buy that shirt."

o   Instead of saying "I *can't* afford to buy that shirt," you could say, "I *choose to* save money *instead*."

o   When you say "I can't," you're telling your subconscious mind that you're incapable of doing something when the truth is usually that you're *choosing* not to do it. Take responsibility for your choice or else your subconscious mind will falsely believe that you're an incapable human being.

– **Replace the words "I might" with either "I will" or "I won't'"**

o For example, instead of saying "I might come to the party tonight," say, "I won't be at the party because I made other plans," or "I will give you an answer by the end of the day."

o The word "might" is incredibly passive—it doesn't give yourself or the recipient any concrete information. You are therefore likely to avoid taking responsibility.

– **Replace the words "I'll try" with either "I will" or "I won't'"**

o   The same rules apply to the word "try" as the word "might."

o   Additionally, if someone compliments you for doing great work, *do not* say, "Thanks, I try!" If someone noticed that you are doing a great job at something, it's clear that you're not *trying* to do a great job, you're *doing* a great job; there's a key distinction. Instead of saying, "I try," simply thank the person and let them know you appreciate it. When you deflect compliments, your subconscious mind will start to believe that you're not worthy of receiving them. That is bullshit. You earned your compliments, so receive them with grace and humility.

- **Replace the words "I hope" with "I am committed to"**

   o   For example, instead of saying, "I hope I write a book," you could say, "I am committed to writing a book."

   o   When you "hope" something happens, you haven't committed to taking responsibility. Hoping something happens is far different than making it happen.

- **Replace the word "but" with "and"**

   o   For example, instead of saying, "I want to start dating but I don't have time," say, "I want to start dating AND I'm going to create time to do so."

   o   When you use the word "but," it prevents you from taking action. The truth is, anything you say after the word "but" is a complete story that you made up. Every time you say I want X but Y, you begin to associate the thing you want most (X) with the consequences (Y) when it truly has no connection whatsoever.

   o   Catch the "buts" in your life, kick them out, and take responsibility for your actions.

The formula is simple:
- The clearer your subconscious mind
- The clearer your focus (target)
- The greater the chance you'll hit your target!

Remember, where intention goes, energy flows. **If you don't know what you want, your life will represent that. You will revert back to your comfort zone and subconsciously create what you believe you deserve.** To implement what you learned in this chapter, think about the obvious things that you want, like better health or finances. We are going to identify your biggest limiting beliefs in these areas of your life and then flip them to create empowering incantations.

The idea behind incantations is that, when you repeat empowering phrases over and over, your mind starts to believe them. The opposite is also true; when you repeat negative phrases over and over, your mind starts to believe them.

The reason why it's helpful to create in**CAN**tations is because most people live their lives believing in their in**CANT**ations, or negative limiting beliefs. For example, a common inCANTation is, "I am not worthy of love." This belief will run a vicious cycle through your mind and reinforce itself through the cycle of beliefs → behavior → results whether you're aware of it or not; the end result is loneliness. Remember how I told you that your results are a direct reflection of your beliefs? Well, in order to live a kickass life, you need a kickass set of beliefs—let's create incantations now to catalyze the process.

Activity:

Write down one of your biggest limiting beliefs.
For example, I am afraid to start my own business, or I am not strong enough to exercise.

_____

_____

_____

_____

_____

Now cross out that belief, laugh at how stupid it is, and write in big letters, "THAT IS COMPLETE BULLSHIT!"

Now write down the antithesis, or opposite, of that belief.
For example, I am excited to start my own business, or I am strong enough to achieve anything I set my mind to.

_____

_____

_____

_____

Enforce this belief by reciting it every day. If your old, bullshit limiting belief (or inCANTation) creeps up on you, immediately replace it with this inCANtation.

Write down another one of your biggest limiting beliefs.

_____

_____

_____

_____

Now cross out that belief, laugh at how stupid it is, and write in big letters, "THAT IS COMPLETE BULLSHIT!"

Now write down the antithesis, or opposite, of that belief.

_____

_____

_____

_____

Enforce this belief by reciting it every day. If your old, bullshit limiting belief (or inCANTation) creeps up on you, immediately replace it with this inCANtation.

Write down another one of your biggest limiting beliefs.

_____

_____

_____

_____

Now cross out that belief, laugh at how stupid it is, and write in big letters, "THAT IS COMPLETE BULLSHIT!"

Now write down the antithesis, or opposite, of that belief.

_____

_____

_____

_____

Enforce this belief by reciting it every day. If your old, bullshit limiting belief (or inCANTation) creeps up on you, immediately replace it with this inCANtation.

These incantations are your friends. Recite them in front of the mirror each morning and repeat them as you go to sleep each night; they will stir into your subconscious mind and plant powerful seeds overnight. Your subconscious mind never sleeps, so be sure to influence it with empowering language!

7.

CHANGE YOUR IDENTITY

"Let today be the day you give up who you've been for who you can become."
—Dalai Lama

THE STRONGEST force in the human nervous system is to remain consistent with your identity. Your identity is a set of beliefs about who you are and what you're capable of. These beliefs can empower or disempower you.

Let's enter a hypothetical situation for a moment...

Let's say you're unhappy with your body so you tell yourself you'll start a diet on Monday. You might have good intentions to start your diet, but once Monday rolls around, you break your word.

There are major consequences to this type of behavior: every time you claim you'll go on a diet and don't follow through, you condition that pattern. Thus, whenever you try to go on a diet again, you fail because you've programmed yourself to fail based upon past conditioning.

You've therefore created a set of beliefs about who you are—an identity—that indicates that you're a person who doesn't succeed at dieting. Thus, anytime you start a diet, your brain anticipates that you will fail before you even begin, which is exactly why you do!

Like I said before, the strongest force within the human nervous system is to remain consistent with your identity. Thus, even if you have the best intentions to reach a specific goal, your brain will find any way to sabotage your progress if it doesn't align with who you believe you are.

Your brain doesn't do this because it's a big fat jerk; it does this because your identity runs the show. Therefore, if you don't believe you'll succeed (even at a subconscious level), your brain will prove you right. Remember how we discussed that you attract what you focus on? Well, if you focus on failure, then don't even bother; you've already failed. This pattern will show up in your life across many different contexts until you learn how to break it.

I just referenced an example of a negative identity belief, but you also have positive identity beliefs. For example, you might have positive identity beliefs like, "I am a hard worker," or "I am a philanthropist," and as a result, you consistently work hard and contribute to others! These are great identity beliefs to have, particularly if you're a single male around the age of 26 who is looking to date a phenomenal young woman (hint, hint: call me).

Some of your identity beliefs serve you, but many don't. In order to dominate life, you must first change your identity. You must realize that **your behaviors are not *you*—they are just patterns.** Until you break these patterns, you will try to create new possibilities in your life but the mess will keep following you. Clean up that mess now by becoming aware of *what* your patterns are and *when* they take place. Once you become aware, break the patterns that don't serve you and replace them with empowering alternatives that do.

Let's create a new identity. Think about something you've really wanted in life but you've prevented yourself from getting it. What do you really want but you've avoided taking responsibility for? Picture it in detail then paint a picture in words below.

Activity:

1. What is something specific that you want in a particular area of life *(i.e., to shed 30 pounds and keep it off, or to pay off all credit card debt)*?

_____

_____

_____

_____

_____

_____

_____

_____

_____

_____

_____

Now ask yourself, "In order to accomplish this goal, who do I need to be that I'm not being now?" I call this your Higher Self. Your Higher Self is essentially the most badass version of yourself.

2. Who do you need to be that you're not being now (in order to achieve #1)?

For example, what characteristics would you take on? What would you need to focus on or believe? How would you need to carry yourself?

_____

_____

_____

_____

_____

_____

_____

_____

_____

3. Give this person a name that fires you up *(i.e., Bosswoman, Superman, Warrior Goddess, The Truth, etc.—make your own!)*:

_____

_____

4. What would (response from #3) do in order to achieve your goal (response from #1)?

_____

_____

_____

_____

_____

_____

_____

_____

5. Rewrite this phrase on the line below:

"From here on out, I am committed to taking actions that are congruent with who (*response from #3*) is. I AM (*RESPONSE FROM #3*)."

_____

_____

_____

Since you've changed your identity, you get to take on all of the characteristics of your new identity (*response from #2*) and ditch all the patterns that haven't served you in the past.

For example, if you're not happy with your physical body but you snack late at night, break the pattern today. Find something proactive to do instead of snacking late at night. Are you eating because you're bored? Meet that need with an empowering alternative. If you're bored and want entertainment, then read a new book instead. Pay close attention to your patterns and break them with alternatives that align with your new identity. Condition it; do it over and over until it sticks.

At first, it may seem challenging to disassociate with old patterns. Let's face it, you're so conditioned to behave the way you do. The more you condition positive changes, however, the more habitual they will become. When something becomes a habit, you start to do it unconsciously—without thinking about it (better known as unconscious competence).

The goal is to condition your new and empowering behaviors so frequently that you don't even realize you're consistently dominating life—it's just who you are; it's your identity.

When you have a tough decision to make, check in to see if it aligns with your Higher Self. Ask yourself, "Would (*response from #3*) do this?" If not, then replace the disempowering old pattern with an empowering new pattern.

Remember that you already are (*response from #3*) right now; you just need to condition new patterns until your results prove it. If at any point you lose traction and hit a plateau, get re-associated with (*response from #3*) by going through the activity above again. Always remember, **all you need is within you now.**

Now that you've learned about the power of your subconscious mind and you're in the process of creating a new identity, let's instill powerful rituals to make the changes real.

8.

Rituals to Run The Game

"Show me your results and I'll tell you your rituals."
—Tony Robbins

ALMOST EVERYONE wants a quick fix to achieve results, and that's why the majority of people in this world are broke, out of shape, and settling for a laundry list of other characteristics that are far beneath their potential. The weight-loss industry is a multi-billion dollar industry because they are the masters of inventing quick fixes. Their glamorous marketing strategies reel consumers in like fish. Most quick-fix approaches aren't healthy, but some are, like juice cleanses.

...But if you're thirty pounds overweight and you think drinking juice for two days is going to override the poor decisions you make during the other five days of the week, you're severely disillusioned. It just doesn't add up. The bottom line is, your body is a reflection of the consistent action you take. You've developed a set of habits for how you treat your body, better known as rituals. This doesn't just apply to your body—this applies to every aspect of your life.

Aristotle said it best, *"We are what we repeatedly do. Excellence, then, is not an act, it's a habit."*

We condition ourselves to behave certain types of ways whether we realize it or not. We can condition ourselves to drive to the closest fast food restaurant when we're stressed or we can condition ourselves to go for a run. The truth is, the actions we take consistently are our rituals. If you look at a middle-aged woman with a toned physique, she looks the way she does because she's developed a ritual to exercise. When she doesn't exercise, she feels totally thrown off because it's inconsistent with her identity to *not* exercise. As a result, she looks excellent because she's committed to excellent rituals. The bottom line is, **you produce consistent results when you implement the same rituals consistently.**

The beautiful thing about the mind is that you can condition it to create the results that you desire most. Again, look at your body, finances, relationships, or any areas in your life that you want to improve upon. Once you determine what you want, you can create a ritual to improve your fulfillment in those areas of life. For example, if you're not spiritually satisfied, you could pray or meditate every day. If you want to improve your finances, you can create a budget and assess your spending once a week. Whatever you want most in life, there's always a ritual that will bring you closer to your goal. Create a schedule for your rituals and stick to them.

For example, my friend Blake is an entrepreneur and he's very well known on YouTube. He told me that when he started making YouTube videos, they barely picked up any traction (about one to two subscribers per week). Oftentimes, he wondered what the hell he was doing and why the hell he even bothered, but he made the decision to post videos consistently regardless of the outcome. He created a schedule for when he would post and he stuck to it. After about eight months of uploading videos consistently, Blake's presence on YouTube started picking up until it completely took off. He is now one of the most searched posture and corrective exercise experts on YouTube and owns a lucrative online fitness business that is flooded with clients from his YouTube channel; talk about a powerful ritual!

The bottom line is, the actions you take consistently produce your results. Thus, if the results you're producing aren't bringing you closer to your goals, simply change your approach. Change your approach until you produce the results you want—then turn that approach into a ritual that you do consistently. Think of your rituals as a system for success: **when you consistently use a successful system, you consistently produce successful results.**

According to the research study, *How Are Habits Formed: Modeling Habit Formation in the Real World,* it takes 66 days on average to form a new habit.[5] Habits are similar to rituals—they're something done repeatedly until they become an intrinsic part of your identity. To dominate life, you need to have excellent rituals in place. For optimal results, stick to your rituals over the next 66 days and find a way to measure the changes they produce in your life. If your rituals bring you closer to your goals, keep following them. If they're taking you further away from your goals or your progress plateaus, develop new rituals or tweak the existing ones until they produce the results you want consistently. The bottom line is you need to create momentum on a regular basis in order to dominate life. Let's create some rituals now, shall we?

Activity:

What rituals could you implement into your life to produce better results (*i.e., daily exercise, regular meal preparation, meditation, daily journaling, etc.*)**?**

---

[5]Lally, Phillippa, et al. "How Are Habits Formed: Modelling Habit Formation in the Real World." *European Journal of Psychology* 40.6 (2009): 998-1009. *Wiley Editing Services.* Web. 19 Jul. 2016.

List three rituals below.
Remember to start out with very simple rituals, like packing your lunch every day or making a gratitude list each morning. As you consistently produce better results, you can crank your rituals up to the next level. Again, keep it simple for now so you're certain you will commit.

1.

_____

_____

2.

_____

_____

3.

_____

_____

When will you do these rituals (ex., morning before breakfast, at night before bed, etc.)?

1.

_____

_____

2.

_____

_____

3.

_____

_____

Talk is cheap until it's backed up by action, so schedule your rituals into your calendar to make the commitment real. Many people say, "I'll start going to the gym someday," or "I'll begin meditating someday," but "someday" is not on the calendar. Turn your "shoulds" into "musts;" schedule your commitments now to ensure you take action as soon as possible.

9.

TO SEE IS TO BELIEVE.

"I dream my painting and paint my dream."
—Vincent Van Gogh

MEDITATION is a powerful tool you can use to connect with your Higher Self. It helps you get calm, clear, and connected to your bigger purpose in life. Some people believe meditation is "woo-woo," but it's becoming increasingly more common as more and more research reveals its profound effects on the brain.

The National Institutes of Health, a medical research agency of the US government, funded over 20 studies on meditation. Their research proved that a small amount of daily meditation, in the range of fifteen to twenty minutes a day, actually alters the size of portions of the brain, the blood flow in the brain, and what parts of the brain are active in any given situation. This suggests that meditation can actually "re-wire" your brain structure.

Researchers at Massachusetts General Hospital took MR images of 16 participants before and after an eight-week meditation-based mindfulness program. The analysis of the MR images found increased grey-matter density in the hippocampus, known to be important for learning and memory, and in structures associated with self-awareness, compassion and introspection.[6] This shows that mediation plays an active role in enhancing your quality of life and well-being.

Meditation helps you connect with who you truly are. Let's face it, a lot of people are guilty for seeking outside of themselves for answers. They might ask their friends or families for advice when they feel conflicted or they might read books and attend seminars. You might have done this in the past, too, but the bottom line is, **no one knows the path to your truth but you.** Meditation is a powerful way to reveal your truth.

Think about your mind like it's an antenna. The messages it receives are often interrupted with static. When you meditate, the static clears away. This is when you have the opportunity to hear your whispers of wisdom. You whispers of wisdom are guided messages that come from within; they are

---

[6]McGreevey, Sue. *Eight Weeks to a Better Brain:* Meditation Study Shows Changes Associated with Awareness, Stress. Harvard Gazette, 2011. Web. 19 Jul. 2016

truest in nature to who you are. You can only hear them when your antenna is clear.

So when you feel lost and don't know what to do, just get still. Remember, all that you need is within you now. Tune into your whispers of wisdom by developing a meditative practice and sticking to it each day.

Visualization:

There are many forms of meditation; visualization is undoubtedly one of the most powerful. Visualization is a form of meditation in which you create deliberate imagery in your mind. Visualization is so powerful because it gives you the ability to see your dreams in your consciousness before they materialize into existence. It's simple; all you do is imagine whatever you want in detail and turn it into an experience in your mind. It's almost like you're dreaming except you're in complete control of what you choose to imagine.

Visualization is so powerful because the more you associate with what you want, the more real it becomes—even if it's in your mind. Like I said before, your subconscious mind is like a three-year-old child; it cannot differentiate reality from what you vividly imagine. Remember how our good friend the reticular activating system (RAS) seeks out what it's looking for? **When you introduce your imagination to new possibilities, they begin to take shape in the outer world.**

How to Visualize:

First off, you can't visualize once and expect permanent results; it should be a ritual. To dominate life, develop a meditative practice and do it every day (you can visualize or develop your own practice). The more consistent you are, the greater the opportunity you'll have to rewire your brain in favor of shifting your identity and creating the compelling future you desire.

Think big; visualize whatever you want. Think about it, you can't decorate a magnificent room without having a vision for what the room will look like first. The same holds true for your life—you can't create the life you want if you don't have a clear vision of what it looks like. So visualize what you want as though you already have it now and you will begin to create it in reality!

Visualization might be new and different to you. You might be concerned that mystical fairy unicorns will appear out of the woodworks, fly around your bedroom, and poop glitter on your head. I assure you this won't happen (*but if it does, please consult with a psychiatrist*).

The point is, it might seem different, but different is exciting. Let's face it, if you keep doing the same things you've been doing, you'll keep getting the same results you've been getting. You wouldn't be reading this book if you wanted your life to stay the same, so I invite you to give visualization a whirl and see what happens.

What's great about visualization is that it's the most proactive thing you can do while sitting on your ass. It's so simple; all you do sit down, close your eyes, and set intentions. Direct your mind wherever you want it to go and fully associate with your vision as though it's happening right now. **With just ten minutes of visualization today, you get to choose who you will become tomorrow**; it's like casting a hook into your future and pulling your vision towards you.

If you're new to visualizing, don't worry. It took me a while to figure out what worked best for me, but once I figured it out, my practice became more incredible each day. The process is simple. Find a quiet place to go. Sit in a position that is comfortable, but not so comfortable to the point that you fall asleep. The traditional style for meditation is to sit cross-legged with your spine erect and your palms resting on your lap facing upward (as to receive energy from God, the universe, mystical fairy unicorns, etc.). You're a grown-ass adult, though, so sit however you want.

When you visualize, it is very important that you tune out all distractions. Switch your phone into airplane mode and set a peaceful alarm if needed. Visualize for *at least* ten minutes each day. If you want to go longer, do it. It's open to interpretation. That's the beauty of it.

Be still. Be silent. Settle your thoughts. Settle your mind. Take a deep breath in through your nose and out through your mouth. Inhale as much air into your lungs as you can, and exhale as much as you can through your mouth. Do this five or more times until you feel completely centered.

Take your mind wherever you want it to go. A great way to start is by visualizing your ideal day. Walk through it in detail. Like I said, the subconscious mind cannot differentiate your reality from your imagination, so the more you see and experience what you want—even if it's in your mind—the more you will attract it in real life.

It's important to integrate as many senses as you can while you visualize. When you engage more senses at once, you connect more pathways in your brain. The three main senses you can integrate during your visualization include sights (visual), sounds (auditory), and feelings/emotions/touch (kinesthetic). The two other senses are taste (gustatory) and scent (olfactory), which can be challenging to visualize, but it's possible if you're a spiritual Jedi. Focus on integrating the first three senses for now. If you choose to integrate all five, then party on, rockstar!

To integrate the sights, sounds, and feelings of your visualization, it's powerful to future pace. Future pacing is when you visualize your future as if it's a movie. The cool thing about this movie is that you're the main character. Make the movie a five-star film. See yourself achieving a major accomplishment in your life. What do you see? How does it look? How does it feel? Who are the co-stars in your movie? What is going on that is so incredible? Tell someone in the movie about the awesome accomplishment you just achieved; listen to the person or people you love as they celebrate your accomplishment with you. Integrate as many senses as you can to create a lasting impression of this powerful experience in your subconscious mind. Condition it each day; visualize the person you want to become until it's who you are now!

Activity:

Give visualization a go! Visualize your ideal day and associate with it as though you're living it now.

10.

DECIDE TO DOMINATE.

"Once you make a decision, the universe conspires to make it happen."
—*Ralph Waldo Emerson*

YOUR MOMENTS of destiny are shaped in an instant. Some decisions involve a lot of thought, but decisions are ultimately made in an instant. For example, once you say the words, "I do," or "it's over," or "I quit," your entire life changes. To dominate life, you must decide what you want then take massive action until you get it. You are about to make some very exciting decisions about your destiny. Before you can create a blueprint for your destiny, however, you must ensure that your path is 100% congruent with who you are.

11.

DO YOU.

*"To love oneself is the beginning of a life-long romance.
"—Oscar Wilde*

IN ORDER TO dominate life, you've got to be 100% congruent; you've got to do you.

When you were born, all of life was a possibility. As you grew up, however, you started to inherit the desire to look good and avoid looking bad. As soon as this process began, you got stuck in a trap of society's "norms." You suddenly stopped doing things like dancing in the supermarket, playing silly games, or saying what you really thought. There were a lot of things you stopped doing because it "wasn't normal." If you continue down this path, you'll be one of the billions of wet noodles on this planet. This isn't in the cards for you, though; you were created for something much bigger than you even realize. In order for you to become the leader you were created to be, you must be yourself.

The truth is, everyone has fears and insecurities—even the people that you look up to. There are so many people in this world trying to become a "me too" public figure, but it's like buying a blatantly fake Gucci purse; shit is tacky.

The world doesn't need another Oprah, Jay-Z, Ellen DeGeneres, Beyonce, Tony Robbins, Gary Vaynerchuk, etc. The world needs you!

Embrace the good, the bad, the pretty, and the ugly—because all of these things combined are uniquely _you_. Never dilute or undermine who you are. You know you're a badass, so cut the bullshit and own it.

Humanity is like a massive puzzle, each human representing a piece of the puzzle. Each person offers different dimensions, but all of the pieces come together collectively to create a bigger picture. We couldn't do this alone. You're a necessary piece of the puzzle. Humanity needs you and all of your wonderful dimensions. If you try to replicate another piece, you're screwing up the bigger picture. Just do you!

If there's anything this book can teach you, it's to be more of yourself. You might be worried about what other people are going to think about you once you get the courage to be the _real_ you. The truth is, **it's none of your business what other people think about you.** Let's face it, not everyone is going to like you. Even if you tried to get everyone to like you, some people still wouldn't, so you might as well just be yourself. As long as you're being the best person you can be, you have nothing to prove. *That* sperm hit *that* egg. Go on with your bad self.

Give yourself permission, today, to embrace your truth.

If you feel lost and don't know what to offer, just offer yourself. And every morning when you wake up, ask yourself, **"How can I add the most value to the world just being myself?"** Then go do that thing; because no one else can do it just like you.

To declare your awesomeness, make a list of reasons why you love yourself. I've made this list when I've been dumped, fired, when I've feel lost, when my father died, and for no reasons other than to put gas in my tank. It works like a charm every time.

The rules are simple—just list as many reasons why you kick ass. Get the creative juices flowing. What sets you apart as unique? What are your best personality traits? Are you intelligent, sexy, resourceful, creative, funny, and supportive? List every single reason why you kick ass. Use as many adjectives as possible to intensify the emotions. The time to be humble is *not* now! Own your epic-ness.

Activity:

20 Reasons Why I Kick Ass:

1. _____
2. _____
3. _____
4. _____
5. _____
6. _____
7. _____
8. _____
9. _____
10. _____
11. _____
12. _____
13. _____
14. _____
15. _____
16. _____
17. _____
18. _____
19. _____
20. _____

These are the natural qualities that make you, *you*! Embrace it. This is your own unique recipe of awesomesauce. Share it with the world.

Next, list all of the things that you're really freaking good at.

What have you done that took a lot of courage, but you did anyway? Are you a good friend, mother, partner, chef, skier, conversationalist, listener, or artist? List whatever pops into your head—the first things that come up will be the truest to your heart. Don't judge; just write your responses as fast as you can!

20 Things I'm really freaking good at:

1. _____
2. _____
3. _____
4. _____
5. _____
6. _____
7. _____
8. _____
9. _____
10. _____
11. _____

12. _____

13. _____

14. _____

15. _____

16. _____

17. _____

18. _____

19. _____

20. _____

Do these things more often—these are your true gifts. No matter how bizarre some of them may seem, your unique skillsets will give you the edge that separates you from everyone else. These are also the things you can monetize off of because **if you love the work you do, you never work a day in your life**.

Now that you're fully aware of all of your unique strengths, let's talk about how you can use them to create an impact on the world.

12.

YOUR PURPOSE DEBUNKED

*"Your greatest self has been waiting your whole life;
don't make it wait any longer."*
—Steve Maraboli

I KNOW YOU'RE reading this book because you want to find your purpose—and you will. Before you do, however, I want to inform you that you have more than one purpose. In this chapter, we will discuss how your approach to dominating life can change as long as it's congruent with your personal impact.

According to dictionary.com, the definition for "purpose" is the reason for which something exists, or is done, made, used, etc.[7] There are many reasons

---

[7]"Purpose." Def.1. *Dictionary.com.* Dictionary.com, LLC, Web. 19 Jul. 2016.

why you exist and there are many ways that you can use your skillsets (like the ones you listed on the previous chapter) to create an impact on the world.

The definition for impact is influence; effect.[8] Your impact is more experience-based; it's a "feeling" rather than a "thing." When you get clear of the experience you want to create for yourself and for everyone around you, then your approach can (and probably will) change many times. The bottom line is, **as long as you're aligned with your personal impact, you are on the right path.**

When you're on the right path, you feel a sense of being pulled towards something rather than pushed into it; it doesn't feel forced. You can sometimes enter a "flow" state and lose track of time because you genuinely enjoy doing what you're doing. This is an indication that you're getting closer to where you want to go or that you've already arrived to your destination. Let's take a moment to get clear of your personal impact.

Activity:

What is the impact you want to create on the world?

What's the experience you want to create for others—how do you want to make people feel or what do you want to leave them thinking about after

---

8"Impact." Def.3. *Dictionary.com.* Dictionary.com, LLC, Web. 19 Jul. 2016.

interacting with you? For example, you could make them feel inspired into action, calm and clear, safe and loved, thinking about new possibilities, etc.

_____

_____

_____

_____

_____

_____

Now that you're clear of your impact, there are an infinite number of ways to create it. The point is, you don't have to stick to one "thing" for the rest of your life; that model of living is oppressive and outdated. Instead of sticking to one career for the rest of your life, you can blend all of your unique skillsets (like the ones you listed in the previous chapter) to create the experience (impact) of a lifetime! Who says you can't be an actor turned author turned public speaker? Who says you can't be a computer programmer turned network marketer turned retreat host? Who says you can't be a dancer turned Nutritionist turned traveling taste tester? Of course there will be stepping stones leading towards the bigger picture, but as long as you're aligned with your impact, you can do all of these things *and* feel passionate along the way! Congruence is key.

You already hold the blueprint of what you're capable of being. Humble yourself down and use your unique qualities and skillsets however you see it best serving the good of the planet. Each of us has unlimited potential, and once you make yourself fully available to express your potential, it will flow through you naturally. **You don't have to go out and look for your passion; it is an intrinsic part of who you are.** Once this sinks in, let's take it a step deeper to create a blueprint for life domination.

13.

YOUR MISSION DEFINED

"Have the courage to follow your heart and intuition. They somehow know what you truly want to become."
—*Steve Jobs*

IT'S TIME to get excited! You are about to discover exactly what you want. This is the chapter where you hit the drawing boards and get crystal clear of your purpose and how to achieve it.

Before proceeding, I invite you to enter this process with a completely open mind. The more open-minded you are, the more you will benefit from the activities. I also encourage you to complete the activities in this chapter in one sitting to stay fully connected with your vision.

Think big—crazy big. Steve Jobs said, **"The people who are crazy enough to think they can**

change the world are the ones who do." For example, when Jim Carrey was totally broke, he wrote himself a check for 10 million dollars. Despite the odds, he believed in himself so much that he actually surpassed his goal in one of his earliest major films, *Dumb and Dumber*. This is the exact type of mindset I encourage you to approach this chapter with. Don't place any limitations on yourself. As a matter of fact, get unreasonable in the expectations you set for yourself.

The final belief I want you to adopt for this chapter is the belief that everything pays the same. Oftentimes, people hold themselves back from pursuing their passion because they're afraid that it won't pay the bills. If you're one of those people, please suspend all disbelief. First off, **money can't make you something you already are**. Second off, **with passion comes power, so when you're truly passionate about something, nothing and no one can stop you from reaching monumental heights**. Pretend that everything pays the same so you can align with your innate desires 100%.

It's time to create the blueprint for your compelling future. Just think of how incredible it will feel to finally have a step-by-step guide to follow to your dreams! To make this a reality, I will guide you through my 3-part framework called the Mission Map. The Mission Map was inspired by Tony Robbin's Rapid Planning Method, or RPM; it is a meaningful system of thinking that will dig into both the psychology and strategy behind your goal.

Put your thinking cap on, take out a pen, and get ready to be unreasonable. We are about to explore your deepest-rooted desires and bring them to fruition.

The three parts to the Mission Map include:
1. Mission- your mission is what you want most in life.
2. Motivation- your motivation is the reason why you want it.
3. Momentum- these are the specific action steps you will take to generate momentum towards your goal.

First, let's focus on your mission. Since you can't hit a target you can't see, you must get crystal clear of what you want before you can get it. **Clarity is power.** Think about what you would do if you knew you couldn't fail.

Paint the picture in colorful detail. Make your vision as extraordinary as possible—this is your life we're talking about here! Think about it, what would you do if you knew you couldn't fail? Write down exactly what you would do.

MISSION

1. What would you do if you knew you couldn't fail? Think BIG! Go as big as possible. What would you do if you knew you couldn't fail?

Note: Direct your focus where it currently means most to you. For example, if it means most to you to figure out your career, use this section to describe in detail how you would make a living if you knew you couldn't fail.

_____

_____

_____

_____

_____

_____

_____

_____

_____

_____

_____

_____

_____

_____

_____

_____

_____

You might feel excited about your response and you also might feel a bit overwhelmed because your vision seems massive. That's totally normal; I told you to think big to get your creative juices flowing, but I don't want your vision to be so big that you fall into a state of analysis paralysis.

To get maximum results towards achieving your mission, let's chunk it down into a very tangible goal. Think about this question, "Where do you see yourself in 365 days from now?" Write your response in terms of what you can achieve towards your ultimate mission (your response to #1) within the next 365 days.

2. In relation to your big vision, where do you see yourself in 365 days from now?

_____

_____

_____

_____

_____

_____

_____

_____

_____

_____

Doesn't it feel incredible to see how much you can accomplish towards your goals in one short year?

From here on out, we'll focus on your 365-day vision so that you can build up to your ultimate mission year by year until it's achieved. All of the questions moving forward refer to your 365-day vision.

Once you create your 365-day vision, it's time to check in with your intuition. Your intuition is so important because **you are a spiritual being having a human experience.** The true answers are always within you, but you need to filter through your rational mind's beliefs and opinions in order to unlock access to them.

Look at what you wrote down. Close your eyes and visualize what life will be like once you reach this new milestone. Float forward in time by 365 days and see it as though you've already achieved it. See what you'd see, hear what you'd hear, and really feel the feelings of what it would be like to be living your mission. Like I said before, your subconscious mind can't tell the difference between what you vividly imagine versus what's real, so imagine that you have it all now!

As you explore this visualization, check in with your body. Specifically focus on the response in your gut. Do you feel any sort of resistance in your gut when you imagine achieving your mission? If so, your body is giving you feedback that it isn't truly aligned with what you *believe* you want. If your body reacts with excitement, that's a sign that you are fully aligned to your vision. You'll know you've created the right mission once your body is tingling with excitement and you have a satisfied grin on your face like a stoned Chihuahua.

If you wrote down more than one mission and don't know which is the best option for you, visualize each option as though you've already achieved it. Go through the same visualization process described above. Vividly imagine yourself in each scenario. Whichever options trigger feelings of resistance, cross them off your list! Narrow the list down to the one mission statement that makes you feel like you're being pulled towards it like a magnet!

Once you determine what your mission is and you're totally aligned with it, make it specific. For example, writing "I want to become an English teacher in China by Fall of 2018" is much better than writing "I want to teach English." Finally, write your 365-day vision using language that excites you! For example, instead of saying, "I want to become an English teacher in China by Fall of 2018," you could say "Become a kickass international English teacher in China by Fall of 2018!" Use whatever language resonates with you.

3. Write the specific mission you want to achieve within 365 days *(your response to #2)*, but write it in detail using exciting language!

Summarize your mission into 1-3 sentences to make it a mission statement. This is the final answer you will be running with moving forward, so make sure it truly comes from your heart and energizes you.

Write your final mission statement below.

_____

_____

_____

_____

_____

_____

Now that you have a specific and exciting mission, you must find compelling reasons why you want to achieve your mission. This is so important because **when you have a strong enough reason _why_ you want something, the _how_ tends to take care of itself.** Look at the mission statement that you wrote down. Begin to reflect on why it means so much to you. Give it some purpose. This is going to be the motivation behind everything you do.

Before you get super excited to explore the motivation behind your mission, make sure your mission is 100% congruent to who you are. Ask yourself this question, is your mission truly the mission *you* want, or is it the mission that society or your family wants for you?

For example, when I went to graduate school to get my Masters in Clinical Nutrition, I realized after a few months into the program that I was only going because at some unconscious level, I thought it would make my parents proud. Once I realized my heart wasn't in the program, I dropped out. I don't want you to experience the same challenge I did (it cost me a lot of time and money!). Get realistic with yourself and ask whether or not your aspirations are truly yours or if you're only striving for this mission to prove that you're good enough for others. Check in with your gut. Make sure it's doing a happy dance before you move on to the next step.

If you feel nervous energy, that is normal. If you think about it, your body elicits the same biochemical response when you're stressed as it does when you're excited—your heart beats faster, you breathe rapidly, and you might shout, "Oh, my god! Oh, my god!" **The only difference between nervousness and excitement is the meaning you give it.** Thus, if you feel nervous energy, that's a sign that you are probably excited. If the nervous energy feels uncomfortable in your gut, however, that is a sign that you're not aligned. Keep running through these questions until you find something that feels genuinely exciting and true to who you are. Remember to leave your logical brain in the back seat. Always capture your immediate gut response to these questions, meaning write down your responses without even thinking; these are the truest, most intuitive answers.

Next, take a look to see if your vision serves a higher purpose. What I mean by that is, does your mission only benefit you, or does it benefit humanity on a greater scale? If it's all about you, you'll eventually run out of gas.

For example, when I was a Personal Trainer, I believed that the next logical step in my career was to become a fitness model. I figured modeling would be a great way to market myself, take on more clients, and change more lives. Once I checked in with my intuition, however, I realized that I truly didn't want to become a fitness model whatsoever. As a matter of fact, I would have screwed society over if I became a fitness model because I'm a complete monster when I restrict my diet for long periods of time. I realized the real reason I thought I wanted to become a model was truly for egotistical reasons, which is why I felt totally uninspired to move forward. This explained why I kept hitting Upper Limit Problems and sabotaging my progress without consciously understanding why; there was a major lack of congruence. Once I checked in with my intuition, I realized that I wanted to be respected for my intellect rather than my image. I changed paths by doing what was congruent with my vision—things like writing this book and donating the profits to charity.

The bottom line is, if your mission doesn't serve other people in some way, shape, or form, you will eventually feel like your life lacks meaning. If you want a Ferrari, that's totally awesome. I want one, too...But you need to make sure it's not about the bright and shiny objects; they are just a fun byproduct of the value that you share with the world. **Always look to create things that are bigger than you are**. If you need to edit what you previously wrote down, now is your final opportunity.

Once you are certain that you've picked a mission that inspires you *and* serves the greater good, give it some meaning. Read over your 365-day vision again then answer these questions.

MOTIVATION

1. Why do you feel so passionate about achieving your mission?

_____

_____

_____

_____

_____

_____

_____

_____

2. How would it feel to achieve your mission (in detail)?

_____

_____

_____

_____

_____

_____

3. What would it mean to you to achieve your mission (in detail)?

_____

_____

_____

_____

_____

_____

4. How would this change your life for the best and for those whom are affected by your mission?

_____

_____

_____

_____

_____

_____

5. What does *that* mean to you?

_____

_____

_____

_____

_____

6. Who do you have to be in order to achieve your mission (i.e., who would you be that you're not being now)?

_____

_____

_____

_____

_____

_____

_____

7. Write on the line below, "I choose to be this person right now."

_____

_____

MOMENTUM

You can't steer a parked car—you've got to move! Now that you're clear of the direction you're headed and the driving force behind it, it's time to generate momentum. In this section, you will create the strategy to achieve your mission.

Float forward in time to when you've achieved your 365-day mission. See it as though it's already been done. Once you get a clear picture of the end result, reverse engineer it. How did you achieve this result? What actions did you take to get there?

1. What specific action steps did you take to achieve your mission? Get very detailed and list every step you took. List the action steps below.

_____

_____

_____

_____

_____

_____

_____

_____

_____

Next, add any strategies you think you might need as a backup.
List as many strategies as possible so that if one approach doesn't work, you have several others as backup. This eliminates stress and sets you up to win! Go ahead and add any other momentum steps that you might have missed.

Remember, **results come from action not thought**. The beautiful thing about creating momentum is that it's very simple: just take one step in the right direction. Once you take that step, then take another one. Momentum is merely the act of being in motion—taking action is the only thing that will bring your goals into existence.

As Martin Luther King Jr. said, "**Take the first step in faith. You don't have to see the whole staircase. Just take the first step**." This is a fantastic quote to live by. You don't need to do a million complicated things at once; it's the simple things done consistently that produce the greatest results.

With that in mind, review your list of momentum items and circle the top three items that are the most important in achieving your mission. Meaning, if you just focused on these, you'd almost be guaranteed to achieve your goals.

Next, make your commitment real by scheduling your top three momentum items in your calendar. When achieve one, move onto the next. Some of your momentum items might take place every day, like meditating, for example. That's great. Schedule it. Remember, "someday" is not on the calendar, so when you actually schedule something, it becomes a real commitment; think of it as a date with yourself.

Finally, look at your list and decide which momentum item(s) you can achieve today. Now is the best time to take action towards your mission because you're in a peak state and are fully associated with what you want. Take advantage of your energy while it's high!

Reassess your momentum plan as you need to make adjustments. Remove momentum items that have been completed and add new ones when necessary. Evaluate your progress at the start of each week. If you're getting further from your mission, change your approach. If you're getting closer, continue to build upon what works. Either way, reassess your plan each week to see where you stand in regards to your mission and how you can get there most efficiently.

Once the 365 days are complete, plan your next year keeping your ultimate vision (*your response to #1*) in mind. Congratulations for raising your standards and developing the blueprint for an abundant and fulfilling new life!

14.

ELIMINATE EXCUSES

"You can have results or excuses. Not both."
—Arnold Schwarzenegger

NOW THAT YOU'RE crystal clear of what you want, it's time to eliminate excuses! This means that you **cut off all options except for those that bring you closer to your mission.** Eliminating excuses doesn't mean that challenges won't still show up; they will. There's a solution for that.

In this chapter, you will solve challenges before they happen. More specifically, you'll anticipate any challenges that *might* show up along your journey; you'll create practical solutions in advance.

There are three major benefits to solving problems in advance. The first benefit is that if your first plan fails, you have plenty of backup plans. This gives you complete flexibility in achieving your mission. The second benefit is that flexibility eliminates stress. If you've already anticipated challenges, you won't feel stressed if they show up because you already know how to handle them. The third major benefit of solving problems in advance is that it completely eliminates excuses! When you're already aware of potential roadblocks and you've solved them in advance, excuses cease to exist!

To eliminate excuses, **begin with the end in mind**. Float forward in time by 365 days to when you've fulfilled your mission and see it as though it's happening right now. As you reflect upon your journey over the past year, make a list of the potential challenges that might have shown up along the way.

You might list excuses like, "my family will judge me for changing my career," or " I don't have time to write my book," etc. Whatever your colorful excuses are, solving them ahead of time puts you in complete control. Without anticipating the road ahead, handling challenges would put you in a state of reaction. To dominate life, you must be at cause for your actions. The best way to be at cause (rather than effect) is to anticipate the road ahead.

1. List all of the potential challenges that might have shown up along the way to your 365-day vision. We'll handle the solutions next, but for now just list all of the potential excuses or challenges below. Dump those demons out of your head and put them onto paper!

Excuses/Challenges	Solution(s)

2. For each excuse, list as many solutions as possible. The more the merrier.

If a challenge shows up, you don't have to panic. Just reference the table above to find a solution!

Oftentimes, people get so excited when they set new goals, but when challenges show up, they immediately throw in the towel. To dominate life, **you must remain focused on the outcome at all times.** The truth is, **people will stop over the most trivial things when they're not focused on the outcome.** If a challenge shows up and you find yourself wanting to make excuses, ask yourself, "What's the challenge compared to the ultimate outcome?" Then ask yourself, "Does this even matter right now?"

For example, one of my clients told me she was tempted to eat fast food because she took on additional responsibilities and "didn't have time to eat healthy." She realized that her challenge of "not having time to eat healthy" was trivial compared to her ultimate outcome of having sexy and healthy body. Once she became aware of this, she realized it didn't matter that she had less time to eat because she could actually reach her outcome *and* save time by packing healthy snacks in advance.

Again, when you're clear of what you want and why you want it, you'll find a way to get it. If you begin to create excuses, however, that's a sign that you're losing steam. If that's the case, simply reassociate with your motivation, or the reason why you want to achieve your outcome. Once you figure out the "why," the "how" often takes care of itself.

Finally, people often wonder, *what am I going to **get out of** reaching my goals?* Yet the real question to ask is, *what am I going to **get out of the way to** reach my goals?* Let's be honest, you are often your own worst enemy when it comes to reaching your goals. What I mean by that is, the only thing preventing you from achieving your goals is you. When you give yourself the opportunity to get disempowering beliefs out of the way, you can adopt new beliefs and invent new possibilities for your self and life. (Hint: remember to use those incantations every day!)

One last and very important distinction to remember is **there will never be a perfect time to pursue your dreams.** Many people feel as though they need to learn more before they can start taking action. The truth is, **you don't have to learn more to be ready. No matter how much you know, you will never feel ready**. It's not about all the information you have to gain, but it's about what you do with the itty-bitty nuggets. If you just did half of what you learned, think about where you'd be now. When you put it into that perspective, you'll realize that now is the perfect time to take a leap of faith.

Creating a life by design is an active process; it doesn't happen by waiting for the perfect moment. Throw yourself in the trenches and take imperfect action. This is about stepping up and becoming a leader. In the process, you may make some mistakes. So what? The truth is, you only get one shot. **So many people are treating their lives like this is a practice life, yet this is the real thing**. Focus on the future you want and actively create it now.

Like I said earlier, start with the end in mind. This will give you clarity to create the next best step. You don't have to move mountains in a day. Just take the next best step! And when you step into a room, make sure *Walk* walks in the room, not *Talk*.

Now that you're clear of your vision and how to achieve it, it's a great time to have someone to check in with as you make progress towards your goals. Let's talk about what that looks like next.

15.

GET A COACH

"A coach is someone who tells you what you don't want to hear, who has you see what you don't want to see, so you can be who you have always known you could be."
—Tom Landry

NOW THAT YOU'RE clear of what you want and you've eliminated excuses, it's time to take massive action!

Let's pretend for a moment that your life is a game. It's possible that up until this point, you've been standing on the field waiting for the perfect moment, person, or opportunity to show up before you start to truly play the game. The problem is, as long as you stand there waiting for someone to pass the ball, you have no opportunity to score. To get real results, you've got to get your ass on the field and go where the action is; you've got to go after that ball! To maximize your opportunity to win, now is the best time to get a coach.

Coaches are leaders who inspire their clients to maximize their personal and professional potential through thought-provoking and creative processes; they hold the client responsible and accountable to reach their full potential. The bottom line is, whatever level you're at in life, a great coach will take you to the next one.

Working with a great coach (or coaches) will benefit you in many ways. First, coaches offer incredible perspective. Les Brown said, **"you can't see the picture when you're standing inside the frame."** This means that your coach can see what you can't; he or she will illuminate your blind spots so you can transform what isn't working immediately. Your coach will also bring awareness to your strengths so you can build upon them. The truth is, your coach's perspective will give you a major competitive edge in life.

The next benefit is that a great coach will quickly take you to the top. So many people waste years of their lives trying to reinvent the wheel. They try to figure everything out on their own yet most of them never produce results to show for it. These are the same people who want to do things their way, but if their way worked, they wouldn't be like a hamster in a hamster wheel—running to stay still. Your coach has already achieved what you want to achieve; he or she did all the legwork. All you have to do is model whatever he or she did to become successful.

The third incredible benefit of coaching is accountability. Let's face it, no one cares about your goals as much as you do. I don't say this to sound cynical; I'm sure your loved ones care about your goals, but they don't know what type of commitment it takes behind the scenes to achieve them. A lot of people turn to seminars or books to try to achieve their goals. They learn so much incredible content, but seldom apply it. I am a huge advocate of seminars and books, but until you have someone holding your ass to the fire, you can easily slip through the cracks. Accountability is key.

You might be wondering how to select the right coach. It's simple. Find someone who has already achieved whatever you want most in life—great health, a thriving business, powerful coaching skills, a passionate relationship, etc.—and hire him or her. You don't have to hire the most elite coach in the world—just hire someone who is a step or two above you. If you outgrow your coach, hire a new coach that will bring you to the next level. It's simple.

You might not think you have money for a coach. I get it. I didn't think I did when I hired my first coach, either. If you really don't think you have money, consider this: **what's it costing you to stay where you are?**

Sure, it stings for a moment to reach into your wallet and invest in a coach, but it stings much worse to settle for mediocrity. If you feel like you are compelled to do something bigger with your life but you keep playing small, you will kick yourself later for not doing something about it now. Besides, coaching is an "investment" because you're investing in yourself, so you can get an ROI (return on your investment) as long as you hold your end of the bargain and take action. Not only will you get an ROI, you'll also get an ROE (return on your experience) because you can never "unlearn" what your coach teaches you.

The truth is **you are your greatest asset.** It's not your car, house, or business—it's you. Everything and everyone in your life can come and go, but the one thing you're always guaranteed to have is yourself. When you invest in yourself, you make yourself more valuable. As you become more valuable, you naturally give more value to the world. When you give more value, more value comes back to you; it's money karma!

I personally work with two coaches to improve specific areas of my life that mean the most to me— my health and business. People call me crazy when I tell them this, but I enjoy being called crazy because of this simple principle: **if you do what everyone else does, you'll produce the same results everyone else produces.** Thus, in order to be outstanding, you must out-stand the rest by doing something different. This is why I have coaches. They push me far beyond my perceived limitations and hold me accountable to becoming the best version of myself, which is something I might not have the courage, strategy, or motivation to do on my own.

The bottom line is, hiring a coach proves that you aren't just interested in dominating life, you are *committed* to it.

16.

PEER GROUP

*"You are the average of the five people you spend the
most time with."*
—Jim Rohn

TO FACILITATE DOMINATION, you must
surround yourself with people on the same mission
as you. This is incredibly important because **you
will only rise to the expectations of your peer
group.** If your peer group has lower expectations
than you, you'll lower yours to meet theirs. The
opposite is also true, so it's critical that you find
friends who inspire you to grow into the powerful
person you were created to be.

Befriend powerful people who energize you,
support you, and inspire you to step outside of your
comfort zone. If you already have powerful friends,
it never hurts to have more. Finding them is easy.
First, think about what you want most in life.
Second, think about where people hang out who

have that "thing" or are striving for it just like you are. Third, go to where they hang out. You can join groups, volunteer, take classes, or attend events to connect with like-minded people. When you spend time with people who are on the same mission as you, your powers combine. Together, you create an unstoppable force to be reckoned with.

To find out whether or not your peer group is encouraging you to grow, follow this simple rule: **If you enter a room and you're the smartest** (or wealthiest, or healthiest, etc.) **person in the room, find another room.** This rule is so powerful because it constantly challenges you to stretch yourself.

Another key to domination is to spend less time with Energy Vampires. You know someone is an Energy Vampire when you feel like they're sucking the life out of you. It is very likely that the Energy Vampires in your life don't want to see you succeed because it will threaten their own self-image. When this happens, they will encourage you to play small. If you remain loyal to them, you will live through their low levels of consciousness, but you're far wiser than that.

With that being said, always keep in mind that no one is more or less important than you are. **Every human is programmed for ultimate success.** For example, the tulip was programmed to be a tulip and the rose was programmed to be a rose. The tulip doesn't look at the rose and say, "Dammit, now I can't become a flower because there's already a beautiful rose!" No. The tulip grows into the best version of itself regardless of the rose and creates a beautiful garden along with it. This means that there is enough abundance for all of us. Thus, be sure not to judge the Energy Vampires in your life. If they want to change their lives, they will. **Everyone is on his or her own path, and it's not your job to superimpose your beliefs about the way things "should" be on anyone other than yourself.** You take care of you. A great way to take care of yourself is to manage your environment for optimal success.

To manage your environment for optimal success, let the people in your life know what your goals are and why you're excited about them. Inform them of the changes you'll be making and how their support could help you moving forward. Finally, ask for their support. For example, if you want to get healthier, have a discussion with your spouse or significant other about what you want, why it's important to you, and let them know what changes you'll be making. For example, let him or her know that you won't be filling the pantry with snacks anymore and that you will be waking up earlier than usual to go to the gym. Do not expect the people in your life to change just because you're changing. Again, you take care of you. Own your responsibilities and yours alone. Whatever your agenda is, let the people in your life know about it so they can adjust to the changes you're making and support you best in making your goals happen.

Some of you might feel like you don't have anyone in your life who supports your goals. For example, when you propose an idea to your friends or family, they judge you and call you crazy. If that's the case, it's okay. Remember that your family and friends want to keep you safe. Rather than getting upset with them, appreciate them for caring and then create your own peer group; a peer group that "gets" you. The point of this chapter is to immerse yourself in an environment that supports the shifts you're creating in your life, so do whatever you've got to do to surround yourself with people on the same mission as you.

17.

IT'S PARTY TIME

"Life should not only be lived, it should be celebrated!"
—Osho

NOW THAT YOU'RE clear on where you're going, you have the strategy to get there, and you've taken action, it's time to celebrate!

You're reading this book because you're an Achiever. I admire you for that because I'm one, too. Even though it's awesome to be an Achiever, I notice many of us share one thing in common: we don't always celebrate our achievements because we constantly want to achieve more.

Achievers like you and I tend to treat life like a video game—once we reach a certain level, we want to reach the next. This is the way life should be; we should always set new goals immediately after we achieve our current goals. However, **we must take the time to celebrate our victories or**

129

else they'll all feel meaningless. Like I said a few chapters ago, if you can't find something to appreciate now, you won't find something to appreciate later.

One of my clients is a multi-millionaire and a best-selling author. He told me that when his first book became a #1 best seller, he received the news, grinned for a moment, and immediately began planning to write a better book next time. Since he never took the time to celebrate the success of his first book, he felt totally uninspired to write the second; he admitted it was actually quite painful.

The reason this man came to me for coaching was because he felt completely unfulfilled and wasn't sure why. We identified that the reason why he felt so unfulfilled was because he kept raising his standards so high to the point that they were unreachable. Once he reassociated with the purpose (or motivation) for writing his second book, he started to take action and celebrate each accomplishment along the way. This conditioned him to achieve even more because he felt inspired when he celebrated his progress. As a result, he became unstoppable in every area of life—not only did he crank out another best-selling book, but his business took off and he even found a lovely lady to share his life with. The simple act of celebrating transformed him into a brand new man full of passion, purpose, and excitement.

Whatever goal you achieve, no matter how large or small, make an effort to celebrate your success! Whenever you achieve an action step from your Mission Map, celebrate! I don't care what you do: you can throw a party, treat yourself to a massage, take a day off, have a glass of wine, take a salt bath, smack your ass in front of the mirror, do a sexy dance, etc. The celebration can be small or balls to the wall. Just make sure it's something that energizes you. You want to condition your brain to love the process of achieving, and there's no better conditioning than positive reinforcement. So every time you achieve a goal, celebrate it, enjoy it to the fullest, then get back to business. But first...

Activity:

Write down your top 3 greatest wins so far today:
Note: they can be big wins, like closing a major deal, or smaller wins, like making time for breathing exercises.

1. _____

2. _____

3. _____

When you focus on your accomplishments each day, you'll notice you begin to accomplish more.

18.

OFF INTO THE WILD

"The journey of a thousand miles begins with one step."
—Lao Tzu

IN THIS BOOK, you learned how your mind is programmed to think negatively. You became aware that you created stories that limited your progress—not because you were dumb, but because you unconsciously wanted to be safe. You learned that you have the choice to change your story; you can use the challenges that weighed you down in the past as learning lessons that can help you change the world. You learned to be grateful for those challenges—you wouldn't be the person you are today if they never took place.

You learned how to appreciate the present moment for what it is. You no longer need anything outside of yourself to feel fulfilled because you understand that all you need is within you now. You learned how to be grateful for the present moment and for everything you have in your life that has helped you become the incredible person you are today.

You were introduced to your three-year-old friend, the subconscious mind, who is always eavesdropping on your life and absorbing all of the information within and around you. You also realized that your language has incredible power over your subconscious mind. You learned that you must ask specifically for what you want because your subconscious mind thinks in terms of shapes and pictures and it will see and attract whatever you speak of—even if it's something you don't want. You now know how specific you must be when you think and speak; speak only in terms of what you want.

You learned that the strongest driving force in the human nervous system is to remain consistent with your identity; you've done work to change your identity in a way that empowers you. You've changed your identity by taking consistent action on your rituals, visualizing what you want like it's yours now, and being the type of person who produces those results.

You understand that rituals are necessary when it comes to achieving your goals. It's not the things you do once, twice, or sometimes--it's the actions taken consistently that produce the best results. You understand that a ritual is a system; you can create a ritual for anything you desire most in life.

Whatever you're striving for, create a ritual to make it real; schedule it and make it a "must" rather than a "should."

You understand that in order to dominate life, you must be yourself. You have a unique blend of gifts that no one else on this planet has. Whenever you don't know what to do, just do you. Every morning when you wake up, ask yourself, "How can I add the most value today just being myself?" Then do that thing.

You learned that decisions shape your destiny and it only takes an instant to decide what you want. You can want many things and get them all because you aren't limited to one "purpose." As long as you align with your personal impact, or the experience you strive to create for yourself and others, then you're on the right path. You know that you can be flexible in your approach to fulfilling your impact, yet you also know that you must have a clear starting point. You found your starting point when you created your Mission Map, or the blueprint to make your dreams a reality.

You finally discovered your passion by creating a Mission Map for your life. You answered the question, "What would I do if I knew I couldn't fail?" You chunked your answer down to the next 365 days. This gave you the jumping-off point to determine the strategy you'd use to get yourself there. You visualized your 365-day mission as though it were already done and you reverse engineered it. You captured the momentum steps that you took to achieve your mission. You also became very associated with your motivation behind the goal—or the reason *why* you want what you want. This enabled you to give your mission some fuel so you could easily create the strategies to make your decision real. You decided which strategies on your momentum plan were most important, and you scheduled them in your calendar. You committed to taking each action until you achieved your mission. You understand that you should adjust your 365-day mission plan as you go, and that it should be completely reassessed every 365 days. The training never stops.

Once you were completely committed to your mission, you eliminated excuses. You wrote down every excuse or challenge that *might* show up in the future. You created a practical solution for each in advance. Now if any of those challenges show up, you know exactly how to overcome them because you've already mapped out a plan. This leaves you with room for no excuses!

Once you determined exactly what you wanted and how to make it happen, you learned that a coach will take you to the next level by offering perspective, strategy, and accountability. You know that working with a coach is the quickest way to achieve your goals because you can model his or her success rather than reinventing the wheel on your own time and at your own expense.

Finally, you learned that every time you achieve a goal—no matter how big or small—you must celebrate. Without celebration, life becomes mundane. The best way to motivate yourself to achieve more is to let loose and have some fun when you achieve your goals.

It's been an incredible journey and I'm so grateful that you joined me for the ride. Please know that I love you and I am so excited for you to share your bright light with the world. As you take these first steps out into the wild, remember to enjoy each step. I am with you, supporting you, every step of the way. Now go out there and dominate life!

19.

MY GIFT TO YOU

I WANT TO give you a gift!

I am offering several incredible resources that will set you up to dominate life. Before I do, let me tell you about my fun social media challenge!

Social Media Challenge:

Take a picture of yourself holding this book. Upload your photo to Instagram or Facebook using the hashtag **#dominatelife**

In the caption of your photo, share your biggest takeaway from the book and how you'll apply it to your life moving forward. I review submissions daily!

Each month, I will select one lucky winner to have a 30-minute strategy session with me free of charge. I'll give you the opportunity to receive coaching around something that is very important to you.

To win, all you have to do is take a creative photo with your book (i.e., eccentric, funny, bold, inspiring, etc.), upload it to social media using the hashtag **#dominatelife** and share your biggest takeaway from the book! I will select the monthly winner based upon how moved and/or amused I am by your photo and caption. See you on social media!

Bonus Option 1:

Do you ever feel like you can't commit to a healthy lifestyle no matter how hard you try? This happens because you haven't created an identity that supports you in reaching your health goals. The first bonus, *Train Your Brain for Lasting Health* will help you create an identity that empowers you to achieve long-lasting wellness.
You can download it here:
www.kearapalmay.com/health
Train Your Brain for Lasting Health will help you bridge the gap from where your health is now and where you want it to be. You cannot truly dominate life if you don't have the energy, confidence, or follow-through to do so. Take control of your health and life today by downloading *Train Your Brain for Lasting Health*!

Bonus Option 2:

The second bonus is my 5-step strategy to creating your very own online following and business. If you're an entrepreneur or an aspiring entrepreneur, this is an incredible tool for you! This training will teach you how to transform your business ideas from a concept into a system that creates raving fans!

You can receive the gift now by visiting www.kearapalmay.com/passion

Also, please visit my website:

www.kearapalmay.com

There, you can sign up for my newsletter where I offer regular, ongoing support on how to dominate life and pursue your unique passion to be the leader you were created to be.

When you subscribe to my content, the energy and benefits of this book will continue to empower you to kick ass and take names. Check it out!

Also, please keep up with me on Facebook and let me know what benefits you've received from this book. I'd love you to make posts anytime.

Connect with me:

www.facebook.com/kearapalmay

Finally, I wrote this book with the intention of empowering you; I certainly hope you feel empowered!

...But if you're left empowered and no new action is taken, who cares?

Do you want to die average?

Hell no! "Average" is not who you are.

If you loved the book and want to take your journey to the next level, I would love to be your coach. As your coach, I will hold you responsible to stepping into your full potential.

I have clients from all over the world. I have both one-on-one clients and communities of clients that I work with in groups. Send me an email for special information on my services and allow me to empower you to maximize your greatness.

keara@kearapalmay.com

Thank you so much!

Keara Palmay

ABOUT KEARA

Keara Palmay is a powerful player in the world of transformation. She is an author, motivational speaker, and professional Results Coach. Keara empowers visionaries, entrepreneurs, and revolutionary leaders to maximize their personal and professional potentials. She believes that everyone was put on this planet for a distinct purpose and her purpose is to empower growth-minded millenials to create a compelling vision for their lives and build it into fruition.

With a background in Neurolinguistic Conditioning and Functional Neurology, Keara offers a unique approach to human transformation; she uses both psychology and strategy to condition the mind for long-lasting passion and prosperity. Keep up with Keara Palmay to raise your standards immediately and never look back!

57492700R00085

Made in the USA
Lexington, KY
15 November 2016